HOUSE OF COMMONS   SESSION 1994–95

ENVIRONMENT COMMITTEE

Fourth Report

THE ENVIRONMENTAL IMPACT OF LEISURE ACTIVITIES

Volume I

Report, together with the Proceedings of the Committee
relating to the Report

Ordered by The House of Commons *to be printed*
12 July 1995

LONDON: HMSO
£20.00 net

246-I

The Environment Committee is appointed under Standing Order No. 130 to examine the expenditure, administration and policy of the Department of the Environment and of associated public bodies.

The Committee consists of 11 Members. It has a quorum of three. Unless the House otherwise orders, all Members nominated to the Committee continue to be members of it for the remainder of the Parliament.

The Committee has power:

(a) to send for persons, papers and records, to sit notwithstanding any adjournment of the House, to adjourn from place to place, and to report from time to time;

(b) to appoint specialist advisers either to supply information which is not readily available or to elucidate matters of complexity within the Committee's order of reference;

(c) to communicate to any other such committee and to the Committee of Public Accounts and to the Deregulation Committee their evidence and any other documents relating to matters of common interest; and

(d) to meet concurrently with any other such committee for the purposes of deliberating, taking evidence, or considering draft reports.

The membership of the Committee since its nomination on 13 July 1992 has been as follows:

Mr Andrew F Bennett (elected Chairman 14.12.94)

Mr Peter Ainsworth
(appointed 1.3.93,
discharged 28.11.94)
Mr Robert Ainsworth
(appointed 13.12.93,
discharged 13.6.95)
Mr Kevin Barron
(appointed 26.10.92,
discharged 13.12.93)
Mr John Battle
(discharged 26.10.92)
Mr Roland Boyes
(appointed 26.10.92,
discharged 20.2.95)
Mr Geoffrey Clifton-Brown
Mr John Denham
(appointed 13.12.93)
Mr Den Dover
(appointed 20.3.95)
Mr Harold Elletson
(appointed 1.3.93)
Mr Barry Field
(Chairman 26.10.94–14.12.94)
(discharged 20.3.95)

Helen Jackson
Mr Robert B Jones
(Chairman 13.7.92–26.10.94)
(discharged 27.10.94)
Jane Kennedy
(appointed 13.6.95)
Mr Bill Olner
(appointed 20.2.95)
Sir Irvine Patnick
(appointed 27.10.94)
Mr Tom Pendry
(discharged 26.10.92)
Mr Eric Pickles
(discharged 1.3.93)
Mr Nick Raynsford
(discharged 13.12.93)
Mr Michael Stephen
(appointed 28.11.94)
Mr Gary Streeter
(discharged 1.3.93)
Mr Roy Thomason

The cost of preparing for publication the Shorthand Minutes of Evidence published with this Report was £6,494.04.
The cost ofprinting and publishing this volume is estimated by HMSO at £14,130.

TABLE OF CONTENTS

LIST OF WITNESSES

LIST OF MEMORANDA INCLUDED IN
THE MINUTES OF EVIDENCE

No.   *Page*

LIST OF APPENDICES TO THE MINUTES OF EVIDENCE

No.

1. Memorandum by the Auto-Cycle Union [British Motorcycle Sport]
2. Memorandum by the British Canoe Union
3. Memorandum by the British Cyclo-Cross Association
4. Memorandum by the British Gliding Association
5. Memorandum by the British Hang Gliding and Paragliding Association
6. Memorandum by the British Horse Society
7. Memorandum by the British Microlight Aircraft Association
8. Memorandum by the British Model Flying Association
9. Memorandum by the British Mountaineering Council
10. Memoranda by the British Orienteering Federation
11. Memorandum by the British Railways Board
12. Memorandum by the British Shooting Sports Council
13. Memorandum by the Byways and Bridleways Trust
14. Memorandum by Center Parcs
15. Memorandum by the Cotswold District Council
16. Memorandum by the Cotswold Water Park
17. Supplementary Memorandum by the Cotswold Water Park
18. Memorandum by the Cotswold Water Park Villages Society
19. Memorandum by the Council for National Parks
20. Supplementary Memorandum by the Countryside Commission
21. Memorandum by the Countryside Recreation Network
22. Memorandum by the Cumbria Tourist Board
23. Memorandum by the Cyclists' Touring Club
24. Memorandum by the Dartmoor National Park Authority
25. Memorandum by the English Golf Union
26. Memorandum by the Environment Council
27. Memorandum by the Fell and Rock Climbing Club of the English Lake District
28. Memorandum by the General Aviation Awareness Council
29. Memorandum by the Hampshire Wildlife Trust
30. Memorandum by the Institute of Leisure & Amenity Management
31. Memorandum by the Lake District National Park Authority
32. Memorandum by the London Green Belt Council
33. Supplementary Memorandum by the Motoring Organisations' LARA
    [Land Access & Recreation Association]
34. Memorandum by the National Caving Association
35. Memoranda by the National Federation of Anglers
36. Memorandum by the National Federation of Sea Anglers
37. Memorandum by the National Rivers Authority
38. Memorandum by the National Trust
39. Memorandum by the Natural Environment Research Council

UNPUBLISHED MEMORANDA

Additional memoranda have been received from the following organisations and individuals and have been reported to the House, but to save printing costs they have not been printed and copies have been placed in the House of Commons Library where they may be inspected by Members. Other copies are in the Record Office, House of Lords, and are available to the public for inspection. Requests for inspection should be addressed to the Record Office, House of Lords, London SW1 (telephone 0171 219 3074). Hours of inspection are from 9.30am to 5.00pm on Mondays to Fridays:

Aircraft Owners and Pilots Association
Association of County Councils
Automobile Association
Captain S D S Bailey Royal Navy
British Association for Shooting & Conservation
British Holiday & Home Parks Association Ltd
British Marine Industries Federation
British Orienteering Association
British Trust for Conservation Volunteers
British Water Ski Federation
British Waterways
Caravan Club
Mrs David Cobb
Mr and Mrs Collins
A R Cooper
Countryside Commission
John Cumberland
Denny Lodge Parish Council
Dyfed County Council
East Anglian Trails
Ecurie Royal Oak Motor Club Ltd
English Nature
English Tourist Board
Environment and Development Company
European Paintball Sports Federation
Green Flag International Ltd
Heart of England Tourist Board
Holt Parish Council
Inland Waterways Association
Mrs J Irvine
J Jackson
Doris and Bernard Jones
Lake District National Park Authority
Landscape Design Associates
Lee Valley Regional Park Authority
Leisure and Rural Development Research Group
Marine Ecology and Sailing
Mrs Emma Meredith
Mrs Hilary Miller, University of Greenwich
National Association of Boat Owners
National Caravan Council Ltd
National Caving Association
National Cycle Network and Sustrans
National Farmers' Union
National Trust
New Forest Committee
North York Moors National Park
Oxford Brookes University, Planning Policies Research Group
Poole Harbour Commissioners and Dorset CC Planning Department
Popular Flying Association
Ramblers' Association

Royal Town Planning Institute
Royal Yachting Association
Salmon & Trout Association
Sheffield Centre for Ecology and Environmental Management
Sheffield City Wildlife Trust
Sports Council
Sustainable Tourism World Conference
W G Thomas
Tourism Concern
Colin Tubbs
Tussauds Group
Jack Weaving
Wildfowl and Wetlands Trust
Frederick J Whitehead
Gordon Wordsworth

FOURTH REPORT

THE ENVIRONMENTAL IMPACT OF LEISURE ACTIVITIES

The Environment Committee has agreed to the following Report:

PREFACE

1. *"There is some corner in the English mind that is forever Ambridge"* (David White, New Society, September 1974).

2. Virtually none of the English rural landscape is rural wilderness. The present day environment has been shaped by centuries of taming the land to maximise food production. The use of the countryside for leisure as well as production is also nothing new. What is a modern phenomenon, however, is the use of rural space by large numbers of urban dwellers.

3. To a large extent this has happened because for many urban people, the countryside has become inextricably linked with concepts of "the good life". Historians have documented the way that the rural landscape has become invested with cultural values.[1] As the towns became industrialised and overcrowded, the countryside came to represent the antithesis of all that was seen as ugly and unwholesome—healthy, peaceful and unspoiled. So it has come about that, although the majority of people live in towns, the country has come to be seen as a national heritage and the quintessence of England. As it is expressed in *This Common Inheritance*: "Our countryside and coasts are a central part of our heritage . . . Our landscapes have been an inspiration for centuries for poets, painters and nature lovers. They help us form our sense of national identity".[2] These concepts of the countryside and rural life covertly informed much of the evidence presented to us and were the inescapable background to our own deliberations. They can be found in fears for the disruption of country peacefulness by the "intrusion" of mass visitors, in the concept of rural life as "heritage",[3] in arguments for the "right to roam",[4] and in the language of "threat", "pollution" and "danger" it is so easy to fall into when examining the issues.

4. Obviously these cultural assumptions, and the conflicts they engender between different interest groups, are an essential part of our brief. However, their existence does mean that potential "threats to the countryside" need to be carefully defined. They include: ecological damage which can undermine our national commitment to sustainability; action which is seen to threaten those characteristics which can uniquely be found in the countryside including tranquillity, natural beauty and a sense of being close to nature; to changes which alter the nature of life in rural areas, whether for those who gain their livelihood there or who choose to commute from or retire to rural England.

5. The assessment of these potential environmental threats ranges from the narrowly scientific to issues which are intrinsically subjective. It is essential that attempts to respond to environmental problems identify clearly which type of environmental issue is involved and the reasons why any type of response is being made.

6. This is particularly true in the case of "noisy" sports, "unsightly" footpath erosion, "intrusive" campsites and so on. England is a country of very diverse cultural attitudes, especially those relating to property, civic freedoms, history, heritage and nature. They are very often attached to local and national decision making processes. Many things said and done in the name of sustainability, conservation or concern for the environment are in fact the result of aesthetic considerations—a precise vision of the way the environment should be. Large scale footpath reconstruction, calls to ban noisy recreation in National Parks, the homogenising and "prettifying" of rural villages (what the Council for the Protection of Rural England calls "the brown sign syndrome") may all come into this category. Perceptions about damage and threat should be taken seriously and explored but action restricting any particular activity should be taken only on scientific and planning advice, fully taking into account the wishes and desires of local people, not merely out of a desire to preserve a vision of rural England that may never have existed.

---

[1] For example, Raymond Williams, Alun Howkins and Martin Weiner.
[2] *This Common Inheritance: Britain's Environmental Strategy*, Cm 1200, September 1990.
[3] *Leisure Landscapes: Leisure, Culture and the English Countryside, Challenges and Conflicts*, CPRE, May 1994.
[4] *Ibid.*

SUMMARY OF CONCLUSIONS AND RECOMMENDATIONS

We have not received conclusive evidence that the number of visitors to the countryside has increased significantly in recent years. (Para 18)

We note that according to the balance of evidence we received, compared to other activities, leisure and tourism do not cause significant widespread ecological damage to the countryside. However there is no need for complacency. We believe there are important issues to address, involving transport, rural culture, and leisure management, as well as local conflicts in specific areas. (Para 32)

We also note that the cultural conflicts are just as real as, and sometimes more important than, the physical problems—indeed they are often the root cause of the various tensions and dissatisfactions that are redefined as threats to the environment. (Para 33)

We feel that there is a need for further research to clarify national trends in recreational use, particularly in sport and active recreation in the countryside, which appear to have grown more rapidly than other activities in recent years. We commend the work of the Countryside Recreation Network in promoting research collaboration and suggest it reassess the priority given to work on environmental impacts, and places greater emphasis on developing a programme of work within the agencies to evaluate management initiatives. Given the difficulties in undertaking nationwide surveys of the ecological impact of leisure activities, we urge English Nature to continue to monitor those sites of greatest ecological sensitivity. (Para 37)

We wish to see a reconciliation of the Countryside Commission's trend data, the United Kingdom Day Visitor Survey and the Department of Transport's statistics to produce an authoritative assessment of the use of the car for countryside recreation. (Para 39)

We recommend that the Government carefully examine the mechanism contained in the Wildlife and Countryside Act 1981 whereby Roads Used as Public Paths (RUPPs) have to be reclassified as Byways Open to All Traffic (BOATs) if vehicular rights are shown to have ever existed. Instead, in consultation with all interested parties, they could be reclassified as bridleways or footpaths. We also suggest that "Plain English" guides to this complicated procedure are produced and disseminated to the general public. (Para 47)

The Countryside Commission has endorsed the recommendation of the Edwards Report setting a target for all public rights of way in National Parks to be signposted where they leave the highway and to be free of all obstructions by the end of 1995, and everywhere by the year 2000. We believe these targets must be met. The Government should consider giving priority to the allocation of resources to the National Park Authorities to take on these responsibilities and encourage local authorities to meet their targets by the year 2000. (Para 49)

If demand for marinas should arise in the future we feel efforts should be made to meet it by the development of redundant land (for example dockland) rather than using virgin riverbank or seashore. (Para 53)

We would strongly urge that any made-for-television competitive climbing events feature climbers using artificial rock walls rather than natural sites. (Para 56)

We felt the limits and conditions in the Code of Practice of the National Caving Association with regard to the use of mechanical excavators, the construction of dams, diversions of water courses and the use of explosives are too weak. (Para 57)

We commend the Code of Practice for golf courses designed by English Nature, which we hope will encourage better design and maintenance, and a more natural use of the land. (Para 58)

We recommend that any future proposals for golf courses be subjected to more detailed environmental assessment and scrutiny by planning authorities in order to minimise their impact on sensitive landscapes, to create new wildlife habitats and to improve public access. (Para 58)

We feel that access agreements can contribute to resolving the conflicting interests of walkers, farmers and landowners. We urge the National Park Authorities, local authorities and the Ministry of Agriculture, Fisheries and Food to pursue access agreements with vigour. We believe that access should be significantly increased by the year 2000. (Para 62)

We recommend that design standards for leisure development should be strictly enforced through the planning system to ensure that development is of an appropriate form and material for the local environment. (Para 64)

We feel that it is important that the positive economic impacts of leisure and tourism on rural areas are recognised. (Para 69)

We see no immediate need to impose any general restrictions on leisure activities in order to provide blanket protection for the rural environment. (Para 71)

We recommend that the Department of National Heritage assume a more pro-active role in developing tourism and leisure policies taking into account the environment, rural transport and agriculture. The Department should ensure that the content of its publications reflects this role. (Para 75)

We trust that the Department of National Heritage will ensure that the English Tourist Board's work in promoting environmental good practice to the tourism industry will continue. We note that at present the Board is undertaking a five-year evaluation of the "effect of its interventions in the market." This should include analysis of its effectiveness in promoting good environmental practice. (Para 78)

We recommend that the Department of the Environment, Department of National Heritage, English Tourist Board, Sports Council and Countryside Commission issue a clear and specific joint statement of their relative roles and responsibilities towards leisure and tourism in the countryside. This could be part of the documentation produced in association with the Sports Council's restructuring. (Para 82)

In many ways the work of the National Park Authorities epitomises the management approach that we are advocating. We would like to see this approach extended to other well-used areas of the English countryside. But good management and good conservation are expensive. We believe that funding for these authorities should allow for the necessary investment in good practice which is sustainable and which is in keeping with local scale and needs within available resources. (Para 86)

There has been no common call for major changes in the national Planning Policy Guidance. We feel that an update of PPG 17 to bring it into line with the concept of sustainability is desirable, and we request that this issue and the comments quoted in this Report be addressed by the Department of the Environment in their response to us. (Para 90)

We recommend that the Department of National Heritage assume responsibility for ensuring that the removal of the Sports Council secretariat does not result in the disappearance of the Regional Councils for Sport and Recreation or lead to a deterioration of their effectiveness. (Para 94)

We recommend that new, appropriate sites should be sought for watersports, particularly power-boating, water-skiing and jet-skiing. These sites should be developed close to large urban centres so as to reduce leisure travel with its attendant fumes and congestion. (Para 99)

We would like to see much more emphasis put on positive planning. (Para 100)

We urge planners to recognise that the principle of sustainability in leisure and recreation involves the provision of facilities for all activities, not only for the aesthetically pleasing and non-intrusive ones. We believe that this might be best achieved at regional level without damaging the environment or increasing conflicts between different user groups by identifying sites suitable for noisy and obtrusive activities. Derelict land or land of low amenity value might be developed for leisure use, reducing pressure on existing facilities and to some extent segregating incompatible sporting activities. (Para 102)

It would obviously aid their case if manufacturers of leisure equipment such as power-boats, jet-skis, trail bikes, and so on were to develop quieter motors to minimise disturbance and noise pollution. Efforts should be made to reduce engine noise at the point of manufacture; we would suggest that noise is often a question of image rather than necessity. Organisers of clay pigeon shoots and other "difficult" events have a similar responsibility to recognise the offence their activities cause to others, and to take realistic and effective steps to reduce the disturbance they cause. (Para 104)

We recommend that planning strategies should identify clearly both sites where intrusive activities are to be restricted and sites where such activities are to be permitted or encouraged. We urge the Government to issue appropriate guidance to local authorities on the preparation of structure plans. (Para 105)

In relation to planning policies in the Coastal Zone, we endorse the findings of our predecessors. We believe that progress in this area, while it is to be welcomed, is still too slow. (Para 111)

We note the need to keep forest policy and the impacts of leisure activities upon it under review. (Para 114)

We believe that footpath work should be subject to a consistent code of practice. We endorse the Code produced by a Joint Working Group of the Lake District National Park Authority, English Nature and the National Trust: "The repair and maintenance of paths in open country will be subject to the following considerations:

a) That the repairs are necessary to prevent or ameliorate visual intrusion and environmental damage;

b) Works should be of a high standard of design and implementation using indigenous materials, sympathetic in colour and texture to the immediate surrounding area. Uniformity of construction should be avoided, eg. steps;

c) Techniques used should protect existing vegetation and, normally, only locally occurring plant species should be used in restoration. Non-local species will be acceptable only where necessary as a 'nurse crop', and where natural succession will rapidly result in their disappearance;

d) The more remote the path, the more stringently the criteria for path repairs should be applied. This will be a matter of judgement but, in general, the more remote or wild the location the less acceptable an obviously engineered path will be;

e) Repaired paths should be suitable to the routes used and constructed on a scale appropriate for the intended use as a footpath, bridleway or byway; and

f) Before any repair work is agreed, the question should be asked "is there a better solution?"

The use of waymarks, cairns or other intrusive features, other than those traditionally established on summits and path junctions, will be discouraged.

A sustained commitment of resources to path management will be sought, so that small scale continuous maintenance can replace infrequent major repairs as the normal method of path management." (Para 117)

We also welcome the efforts of the British Upland Footpath Trust to provide funds for the sensitive restoration of upland footpaths. (Para 118)

We hope that the Countryside Commission's consultation on the maintenance of National Trails will allow re-routing, temporary diversions, and the provision of alternative lines of route. (Para 120)

We believe that dog owners should be encouraged to behave responsibly when on rights of way, through the imposition of fines where necessary. (Para 121)

We recommend that an award scheme for guidebooks be set up, one of the criteria for an award being the sustainability of the route. Other criteria could be adequate parking near starting points, good access to public transport and the matching of the quality of paths to the likely numbers of users. The Countryside Commission could take responsibility for the administration of such a scheme. (Para 122)

We urge the Ordnance Survey to cover all areas of National Parks and Areas of Outstanding Natural Beauty by Outdoor Leisure maps in the near future. (Para 123)

We note and commend the key features of the management approach to sustainable use of Poole Harbour, embodied in the Aquatic Management Plan, which are:

— an information base covering the different interests which has been recently extended by survey work on breeding birds and recreational activities;

— a zoning scheme which protects wildlife areas of critical importance but which also makes provision for watersports;

— a willingness to amend this zoning scheme in the light of new evidence and in consultation with users;

— the use of bylaws to enforce the zoning scheme; and

— clear and attractively produced literature which informs users of the regulations and their necessity. (Para 126)

We believe that as part of an integrated management strategy, measures should be taken wherever possible to attract visitors to currently under-used robust sites which fit the "Best Available Place" criteria. (Para 130)

Codes of practice are useful tools. We therefore believe that it is important to get them disseminated to a much wider audience, providing them to those who are not members of a sporting organisation, via guidebooks, leaflets and manuals. Those who write and sell guidebooks and sporting "how to" books; those who manufacture and sell sports equipment; those who instruct learners or lead parties—all these also can, and should, play a part in familiarising their customers with codes of good practice. (Para 133)

We recommend that the Government takes positive steps to encourage the formation of effective partnerships in such areas and that, where the Government is a major landowner, it ensures that Government agencies play a full part in such partnerships. (Para 138)

We commend the consensus building approach and consider that consultation in local management schemes should begin at an early stage to overcome some of the cultural conflicts which overshadow any evidence of the environmental impacts of leisure. When such consultation is entered into, efforts must be made to ensure decisions are taken within a reasonable timescale. (Para 141)

We feel that there are three important criteria upon which to assess the quality of local countryside management schemes:

— They should follow the same general principles as schemes introduced at national and regional level (principles which we suggest elsewhere in this Report);

— They should clearly have primary regard for the area within the scheme, but not ignore the wider effects they may have; and

— After a management scheme is put in place, its effects should be monitored and assessed. (Para 142)

We believe that the Countryside Commission, working in partnership with the Department of Transport, the Rural Development Commission and local groups, should develop its demonstration traffic schemes to assess comprehensively how they tie in with rural transport and whether they meet the needs of local businesses in a range of tourist locations. (Para 146)

We feel that two or three experimental park-and-ride schemes should be set up on a trial basis, perhaps run in conjunction with the experimental traffic restriction schemes we suggest. (Para 147)

As part of a policy to ease pressure on so-called "honeypot" areas and encourage those less well known it may be appropriate for local consideration to be given to charging above cost for some car parks. Likewise signposting to encourage vehicles away when an area is effectively full should be developed. Additional signposting to encourage visitors to less popular areas should be provided. (Para 149)

We believe that National Parks, County Councils, authorities covering Areas of Outstanding Natural Beauty, and all other relevant authorities should develop a rural transport strategy. The aims of such a strategy should include:

— the provision of new sport and leisure facilities as close to good public transport as possible and near to urban areas;

— the development of public transport to eliminate as far as possible the need to use cars for leisure purposes;

— the encouragement of cycling;

— the recognition that leisure traffic might have to be restricted in some places and under some circumstances;

— measures to ensure that lorries and other heavy vehicles are restricted to major routes except for access; and

— the opening up to passenger use of existing railway routes. (Para 150)

Conversely, such strategies should recognise that some people do enjoy looking at scenery from a car window (or, if they are frail or disabled, can only see the countryside this way). The development of good lay-bys and viewpoints would cater for this group. Additionally, some sports and leisure activities necessitate large amounts of equipment and it should be recognised that public transport is unsuitable for groups taking part in these activities. (Para 151)

We believe that the pressure of visitors, in the end, does need to be catered for, managed and acknowledged. Opportunities for car park facilities should match demand and not be used as an artificial control mechanism unless there is a compelling case on environmental and visitor enjoyment grounds. (Para 152)

We feel further efforts should come from Government to encourage local authorities to develop rural transport for leisure purposes within available resources. (Para 154)

We urge rail operators to maintain and improve facilities for carrying cycles on trains, especially in National Parks. (Para 157)

We recommend that retailers of four-wheel drive vehicles, whether new or second-hand, draw purchasers' attention to the Land Access and Recreation Association and its code of conduct for off-road vehicles, and we commend those who already do so. We also recommend that organisations involved in training four-wheel drive users produce a code of practice in consultation with the Land Access and Recreation Association. (Para 160)

We recommend that National Park and Highway authorities initiate collaborative negotiations between motoring organisations, other rights of way users and local communities in seeking management solutions to the use of green lanes before resorting to statutory traffic restrictions. (Para 161)

We believe that codes of practice and a framework of voluntary co-operation are part of the way forward for the management of motorsports in rural areas and we commend all who have established such initiatives. We have to stress, however, that there will be some conflicts until firstly, quieter machines are developed and used and, secondly, a balance is struck between allowing vehicles on legal routes, providing suitable land for informal motorsports, and preventing the illegal use of land elsewhere. (Para 163)

We feel that there is a need to address the issue of permitted rights again, both in terms of noise nuisance and possible environmental damage. We support efforts to introduce a voluntary code of practice with regard to clay pigeon shooting and suggest that it is completed and introduced as soon as practicable. We would suggest that a suitable time to re-examine the system would be after such a Code of Practice has been in place for 12 months and recommend that it is made clear that if many unfavourable submissions are received these rights will be withdrawn. (Para 168)

We commend initiatives to remedy damage caused by leisure activities through voluntary contributions, especially those which relate to a specific project. For example we thought that the "Our Man at the Top" scheme in the Lake District, which collects donations to pay the wages of a footpath restoration worker was particularly worthwhile. We also commend the measures to educate and inform those who donated to this scheme. (Para 170)

Schemes which encourage and enable contributions to be made by industry are also a welcome development (Para 171)

We see a case for voluntary contributions in assisting in the cost of providing visitor facilities and maintenance of scenically important areas. (Para 171)

Leisure time is something people treasure; and spending it in the countryside creates a sense of freedom that relieves weekday stresses. However, we should not forget that how and where we spend our leisure not only affects other people, but may have consequences for the future of the natural environment. (Para 172)

We would like to draw attention to the interpretation of the sustainability principle put forward by the Royal Town Planning Institute in their document "Rural Planning in the 1990s" which refers to the need to:

— adopt the precautionary approach to planning matters likely to have environmental impact;

— consider the ability of the countryside to absorb development without detriment to the social and physical environment;

— preserve the integrity of environmental systems across the full range of their natural distribution;

— promote a self-sustaining rural economy;

— maintain the character of rural communities; and

— ensure that the countryside has its own dynamic and integrity, and is not "simply a contrived facade for the amusement of visitors. (Para 179)

The Government adopted the following environmental objectives in the light of the "Tourism Task Force" Report:

— to support the development of leisure in ways which contribute to, rather than detract from, the quality of our environment;

— to promote environmental quality issues within the leisure industries as well as issues concerned with the quality of their services and products;

— to ensure that all leisure managers become increasingly aware of visitor management techniques and ways of protecting the environment whilst protecting their industry; and

— to encourage and disseminate those forms of tourism, sport and recreation which in themselves aim to safeguard the environment.

We commend these objectives. (Para 184)

With this in mind, the following list draws together some of the written evidence to form principles for the practical application of "Green Tourism":

— Accommodating "leisure uses . . . which cause no significant damage to the resources they use and preferably contribute to their conservation."

— Using the intrinsic nature of an area rather than importing "attractions".

— Encouraging "low impact" tourism requiring minimum development and promoting the understanding of the countryside.

— Developing planning procedures aimed at conserving "environmental resources" rather than consuming them.

— Assessing the environmental impacts of proposed developments.

— Guiding new developments away from sensitive sites to locations where fewer environmental impacts may occur.

— Encouraging designs for tourist developments which are themselves good examples of environmental principles (with, for example, access by public transport, efficient use of energy, water and habitat), drawing attention to these features on site by relevant means.

— Persuading tourist operators that "green" is not only best for the environment but a positive selling point.

— Reusing traditional buildings for tourist accommodation.

— Developing riding, walking and cycling along vehicle-free routes.

— Developing education opportunities.

— Creating public awareness of the problems that can arise out of tourism and leisure.

— Using tourism/tourist sites/information centres etc., to publicise general codes of conduct such as the country code or relevant specialist codes of practice.

— Siting new developments in towns or on the urban fringe, thereby using tourism to assist efforts to control rural traffic.

— Using tourism to open up/restore alternative modes of transport (canals, horsedrawn vehicles, railways, etc.) (Para 185)

The "Best Available Place" for new leisure facilities would be where new facilities:

— are needed;

— are as near to where the main users live as possible;

— use derelict land, or where this is not available, land of the least agricultural, ecological and scenic value; and are developed with regard to the environmental suitability of the site, conducting an environmental assessment or consulting with English Nature where appropriate. (Para 188)

It should also be remembered that many towns and cities have good family facilities in their urban parks. It is important that these are well maintained and policed to keep them safe and pleasant. As the Institute of Leisure Amenity Management recommended, "urban greenspace and open spaces [should be improved] in order that they can provide the experience of the countryside in the town." (Para 189)

INTRODUCTION

7. Cultural stereotypes such as those briefly outlined in the preface, together with increased opportunities for leisure[1] and vastly increased car-ownership,[2] have given rise to fears that, especially in the case of a few prime locations (the so-called "honeypots"), there is a danger that the countryside could be "loved to death."

8. In the winter of 1994, therefore, we decided to investigate this problem. Our terms of reference were to assess:

— to what degree large numbers of visitors, and the pursuit of certain leisure activities, cause harm to the countryside and wildlife;

— how conflicts of interest between conservation, agriculture, public access and local economic development should be addressed;

— whether current planning controls and guidance notes form an adequate safeguard against excessive or inappropriate leisure development in environmentally sensitive areas; and

— options for the development of more sustainable forms of leisure and tourism.

9. We received well over 100 submissions of evidence to the Inquiry, and between 22 February and 10 May 1995 we took evidence from 22 organisations. Bearing in mind the nature of the topic, we felt that it was particularly important also to examine at first hand some of the issues presented to us. For this purpose, we conducted study tours to the Peak District National Park, the New Forest and Poole Harbour areas, the Cotswold Water Park and the Lake District National Park. We also undertook a visit to the Veluwe National Park in the Netherlands in order to examine another European country's approach to these issues. Full accounts of these visits are printed in the Annexes to this Report.

Acknowledgements

10. This Report would not have been possible without the active co-operation of a large number of individuals and groups. We are most grateful to all the witnesses who submitted written evidence, and especially to those who were willing to follow this up by coming to the House of Commons to answer oral questions and discuss the issues with us. Hearty thanks are also due to all those who devoted time and effort to organise our site visits and talk to us on location. Our specialist advisers for this Inquiry were Mr Geoff Broom[3] and Mr Roger Sidaway,[4] and to them we owe special thanks for their technical expertise, advice and assistance.

11. All the evidence presented to this Inquiry is available in the House of Commons Library to Members of Parliament and in the House of Lords Record Office to members of the public. A selection is also included in the second volume of this Report.

---

[1] We have used leisure as an all embracing term to encompass visitors on day trips or staying away from home, and whether they are town or rural dwellers.

[2] See Table 1.

[3] Geoff Broom Associates.

[4] Research and Policy Consultant, Edinburgh.

LEISURE IN THE COUNTRYSIDE

Demand for Leisure in the Countryside

12.   We noted with some surprise that there was little conclusive evidence that the number of visitors to the countryside had increased significantly in recent years. In particular, the National Survey of Countryside Recreation, which looked at the period 1984–91, showed that the overall number of visits made to the countryside had remained constant year on year.[1] The Countryside Commission stated that "The number of visitors to the countryside has grown relatively little since 1977."[2] This runs counter to the popular perception of leisure trends in that period[3] and, seemingly, against what had happened before that date; Countryside Commission figures indicate that summer weekend trips were significantly increasing between 1960 and 1981.[4]

13.   The figures in the tables below illustrate these trends:

TABLE 1
Growth in leisure since 1891[5]

	1891	1951	1971	1991
Population (000s)	27,231	41,159	46,412	48,119
Average working week (hours)	56 to 60	44.8	40.4	40.0
Paid annual holiday (weeks)	'rare'	1 to 2	2	4 plus
Licensed cars (m)	neg.	2.1	10.4	19.7
Foreign holiday-goers (%)	neg.	3	14	30

TABLE 2
Average Weekly Expenditure in the UK on Sports Goods[6]

Year	87	88	89	90	91	92	93
Spending on sports goods as a percentage of total household expenditure	0.22	0.21	0.28	0.21	0.17	0.19	0.24

14.   During this century there has been substantial growth in the population, in tourism and in demand for access to leisure facilities. An increase in paid holiday entitlement has been matched by a reduction in the working week. Improvements in the road network, especially the building of motorways, combined with a massive increase in car ownership, have dramatically shortened journey times and brought some of the most attractive places in the country within the reach of ordinary families. Furthermore, earlier retirement and better health have created a whole new category of leisure users among the young elderly. Of course, at the same time, more people have chosen to spend their annual holiday abroad.

15.   The pace of change has slowed down since 1971, as is evident in Table 1. This would explain the 'tail off' in overall growth noted in the evidence.

16.   Variations (and no clear trends) are also present in visitor numbers for individual sites. Those we show (and we thank all those who assisted us with this exercise) are not selected to be representative of attractions in England as a whole; rather, we have chosen sites in areas which we visited, and which were willing and able to give us accurate figures.

[1] Ev p 7.
[2] Ev p 154.
[3] Ap 5.
[4] *Leisure Landscapes* background papers, CPRE, May 1994.
[5] Source: House of Commons Library.
[6] *Ibid.*

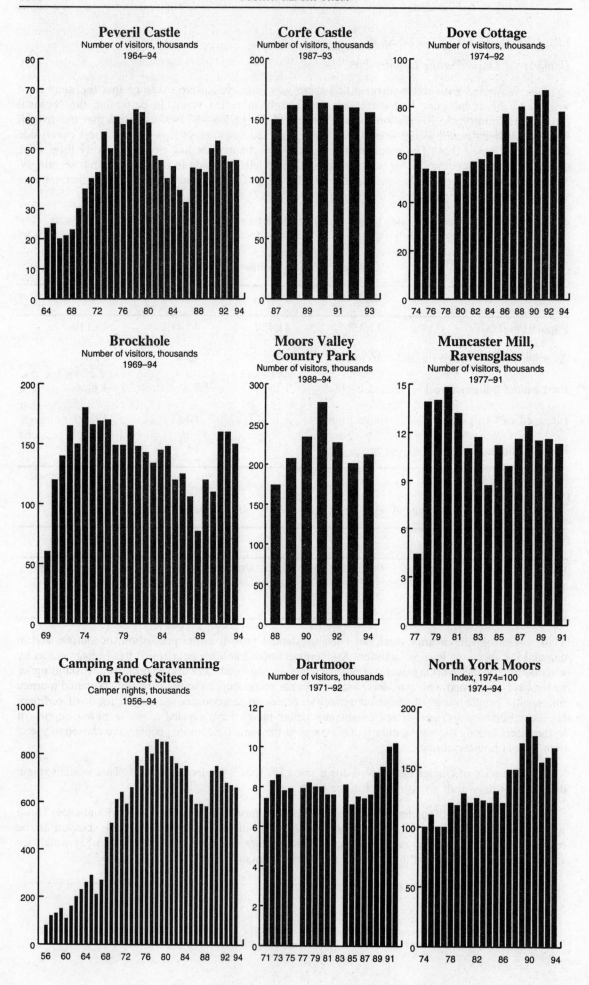

17.   The graphs vary considerably year on year, and do not point to a massive overall growth in visitor numbers. Factors which would affect the figures for particular sites include charging policy, publicity, the weather and even the national curriculum and its effects on school visits. Statistics for sites which do not charge entrance fees are more difficult to obtain; it is possible, of course, that visits to free attractions have increased steadily and indeed drawn visitors away from sites which charge.

18.   **We have not received conclusive evidence that the number of visitors to the countryside has increased significantly in recent years.**

PATTERN AND TYPE OF USE

19.   Witnesses agreed that, although absolute numbers of visitors to the countryside may not be growing rapidly, changes have occurred in the types of activity in which people engage and the pattern of use throughout the year.[1] Less quantifiable leisure activities have also grown in popularity over the last ten years—"destination shopping" to garden centres, markets, car boot sales; and visits to other 'magnets,' for example theme parks and holiday villages where accommodation, all-weather facilities and recreational activities are provided at one site in a prime location. For example, the number of visitors to Alton Towers rose from 1.6 million in 1981 to 2.6 million in 1993.[2] Being unable to second-guess the next fashionable development in the leisure market, it is difficult to predict what will happen in terms of demand and usage in the next ten years or so.

20.   The Department of the Environment's memorandum pointed us towards studies of 'visitor preferences' by the Countryside Commission and summarised that

> "Indications are that a better informed public is looking for new places to visit, and the rise in active sport and recreation during the last 15 years seems likely to continue...The current concern for health and fitness creates a demand for more active leisure opportunities. War games, orienteering, and fitness trails have mushroomed. Tourism studies show similar trends with increasing interest in short breaks. and in holidays which involve active leisure pursuits or special interests."[3]

RURAL TRENDS

21.   Changes in the leisure use of the countryside are taking place against a background of major changes in the rural economy. These have included a rise in the rural population as commuters fulfil their dream of moving into rural areas, entrepreneurs take advantage of new technology to work and live in attractive countryside and people choose to retire to rural villages.[4] The growth in the number of rural residents increases the local recreation pressure on the surrounding countryside.

22.   Changes in agricultural practice have led to a decline in farm employment and created new opportunities for recreation and leisure. Thus there has been an increase in set-aside land—from 2 per cent of English farmland in 1991 to 13.5 per cent in 1994. Some of this has been taken out of agriculture altogether to serve the market for outdoor pursuits,[5] while provision of additional access for walking and informal pursuits has been encouraged by the Ministry of Agriculture, Fisheries and Food. The Countryside Stewardship scheme operated by the Countryside Commission, providing funding for the traditional management of land of particular conservation value, has also provided additional opportunities for leisure use of agricultural land.

---

[1] Ev pp 8, 56, 152.
[2] Information from Social Trends 1995 edition, Central Statistical Office.
[3] Ev p 8.
[4] *Leisure Landscapes: Leisure, Culture and the English Countryside Challenges and Conflicts,* CPRE, May 1994.
[5] See Minutes of Evidence of 3 May (National Farmers Union memorandum).

HISTORICAL CONCERNS ABOUT LEISURE IN THE COUNTRYSIDE

23.   Concern about leisure and tourism in the countryside is not a new phenomenon, as the following quotations show:

"With regard to this question of open spaces, under the present circumstances of this country, increase of population, spread of cities and manufactures, and so on, is it not annually becoming a vital question for the consideration of Parliament?...if England goes on progressing in wealth and population, the probability is that 50 years hence, it will be very much more important to the nation than it is now; and the same remark holds good with regard to all open spaces; the number of people who visit the New Forest in each year is rapidly increasing, and I feel certain that the increase will continue." (1875)[1]

"It is unthinkable that this pleasant land should be allowed to be irreparably defaced. None the less, rapid progress in recent years of urbanisation, the natural ambition of the town worker to have a house in the country or at the sea-side, the break up of large estates for building development; the extension of traffic facilities, the development of industrial undertakings on rural sites, and the eruption, in places of beauty, of ill designed houses and shanties all constitute a real menace to the preservation of its natural beauty." (1929)[2]

"We have pointed out in the preceding chapter that we regard the countryside as the heritage of the whole nation and that it cannot be 'preserved' unless steps are taken to afford those who live in the country adequate opportunities to fulfil their duties as citizens. We point out in Part 1 the not infrequent clash between urban and rural mentalities...We now deal with the conditions which must govern the enjoyment of that countryside, especially by town-dwellers." (1942)[3]

"The greatest threat to the essential character of the area lies in the increased day visitor traffic that may be expected over the next decade. Sheer weight of numbers will inevitably change the tourist 'product' (that is the combination of natural resources such as scenery and transport, accommodation and other services) and raise the question of evolving techniques to manage and direct traffic within the Park." (1965).[4]

LEISURE AND THE ENVIRONMENT

OVERVIEW OF POTENTIAL ENVIRONMENTAL IMPACTS

24.   In this section we highlight some of the potential problems of leisure and tourism which were drawn to our attention by conservation bodies and environmental agencies. The table below, prepared for us by English Nature, is a useful overview of the sort of evidence with which we were presented. In interpreting the table, however, it should be remembered that a 'potential' impact or problem is not an actual one; the fact that damage *may* be caused does not mean that it *necessarily will be*. The table is therefore best treated as a checklist of matters which deserve consideration by policy makers and planners; in itself it does not constitute evidence of threats to the environment.

25.   Other statistics may be found in the table at the back of this Report. It should be noted that some of the statistics in this table are not directly comparable; for example the memberships of governing bodies do not all come from the same year. Additional information about the potential impacts of leisure on the aquatic environment was supplied by the National Rivers Authority. This is printed as part of their evidence in Volume II of this Report. It originates from a 1994 research and development project "to examine the current status of information on the impacts of recreation on wildlife." The project sought specifically to "identify and prioritise those potential conflicts for which further research is required."

---

[1] Report of the Select Committee on the New Forest (1875); Q351 (questions to Mr Fawcett from Lord Eslington).
[2] Report of the National Park Committee (1929).
[3] Report of the Committee on Land Utilisation in Rural Areas, Ministry of Works and Planning, 1942.
[4] Thirteenth Report of the Peak Park Planning Board (year ending 31 March 1965).

SUMMARY OF PHYSICAL AND DISTURBANCE EFFECTS ON SENSITIVE HABITATS AND SPECIES FROM SPECIFIC LEISURE ACTIVITIES

ACTIVITY	SENSITIVE HABITATS/SPECIES	POTENTIAL IMPACT
Aircraft (helicopters, microlights and light aircraft)	Nesting and non-breeding birds Coastal: birds in breeding season	Disturbance to bird populations Potential effects in coastal areas: (a) Increased risk of abandoning/predation of eggs/chicks. Abandoning of breeding sites; (b) Reduction in feeding and roosting time. Energy reserves depleted in search for alternative sites.
Angling	Lakes and rivers; fish and invertebrates; breeding and non-breeding birds	Disturbance to breeding and non-breeding waterbirds and riparian birds; damage to bankside vegetation
Caving/potholing	Cave formations/cave earths; bats	Disturbance to geological features
Climbing	Geological and geomorphological formations; cliff nesting birds	Removal of vegetation; disturbance to nesting birds
Golf	Lowland grassland/heathland	Demand for water abstraction; habitat modification; fertiliser use; cutting management; ancillary development
Mountain biking	Sensitive vegetation/soil types (eg peat, especially in wet conditions)	Localised damage to vegetation and in some cases erosion; conflict with other users
Off-road vehicles (4×4 and trail bikes)	Lowland heathland; lowland grassland; Birds Coastal: Effects on birds during breeding season, wintering and passage. 1. Shingle; 2. Sand dunes; 3. Saltmarshes; 4. Maritime grassland and heath, beaches	Damage to vegetation; conflict with other users See (a) above (more localised) See (b) above (more localised). 1. Destruction of shingle vegetation and of geomorphological structure (irreversible); 2. Destruction of dune vegetation and initiation of erosion (reversible but erosion can be widespread); 3. Localised destruction of vegetation; and, in some cases, erosion; 4. As for 3 above (but less significant/widespread)
Orienteering	Woodland	Localised damage
Paintball games	Woodland	Trampling and erosion; vegetation loss; ancillary development
Riding	Lowland heathland; lowland grassland; woodland	Trampling and erosion; vegetation loss. Also effects as for trail riding and 4×4s.
Walking and dogs	Upland and lowland heath; chalk/limestone grassland; montane heath; mire and carr; breeding birds Coastal: 1. Effects on birds during breeding season, wintering and passage; 2. Any habitat on seawalls; 3. Sand dune communities	Localised damage to upland vegetation on key routes and in some cases erosion; disturbance by dogs (eg. to sheep grazing lowland semi-natural habitats); disturbance to breeding birds. Coastal effects on birds: see (a) above (more localised); see (b) above (more localised) Coastal: 1. Localised trampling and erosion (may not be significant; except on cliff top paths, due to narrow, linear nature of habitat); 2. Damage to seawall vegetation
Water sports	Lakes and inland waterbodies; birds Coastal: All year	Disturbance to breeding and non-breeding birds
Small, powered craft: jet-ski, power-boats, water-skiing, Sailboarding	All year	Disturbance to birds feeding and roosting and to seal colonies
Wildfowling (coastal)	Passage Wintering	Localised disturbance to feeding and roosting birds Death of quarry species
General beach recreation	Summer Cliff tops, shingle, sand dunes	Public use of beaches in breeding season (April-July) limits sites available to some birds eg terns, little ringed plover, oystercatcher Localised erosion leading to: 1. Destabilisation of dunes; 2. Loss/modification of cliff top grasslands through trampling, leading to erosion; 3. Preventing shingle plants completing life cycle eg shore dock, sea pea. Trampling limits the distribution of shingle vegetation, not the geomorphological structure.

26.   We were told by a number of witnesses that the impact of a particular activity depended on a number of factors, including the geology and the flora and fauna present, the time of year, the recent weather and perhaps most importantly the behaviour of the individual participant.[1] The possible benefits to the countryside may also vary considerably between two activities which appear to be almost identical.

27.   It is vital to regard any information on potential impacts in context. For example:

> Visiting group A arrive midweek on a fine day after ten days of dry weather. They pay to park in the village car park, walk seven miles over dry footpaths, visit a historic church, where they buy a guidebook and make a small donation, stop for a drink and pub lunch and buy ice creams and postcards at the end of the day. In contrast, visiting group B arrive on a damp bank holiday after two or three days of heavy rain. The village car park is full so with difficulty they slide their car on to a grass verge. Walking the same route as the As they find that they are churning up mud on many of the paths or having to walk on the soft grass verge to avoid a quagmire. They use the church porch as a shelter to eat their packed lunch, and inevitably leave muddy boot marks and a few crumbs behind them. They leave the remains of their packed lunch in the village litter bin. They return to their car having spent nothing, and join the queue of traffic homeward bound.

28.   It should be noted that personal views can also colour people's perception of what environmental effect an activity is having.[2] Disagreements between those who engage in different activities in the same locality, and between villagers and visitors, are often social rather than environmental, but one argument tends to be expressed in terms of the other. The following extracts from the evidence illustrate these points:

"Not all farmers welcome the idea of bringing the public onto the farm"[3]

"[For 60 years] it has been an objective . . . to secure a legal right of passage over . . . open country . . . mountain and moorland"[4]

"[With regard to tourists] "The sun brings them out like summer flies"[5]

"If all they want is a pub lunch or 'nick-knacks' then there are less environmentally sensitive areas where these can be obtained"[6]

"My family have followed this way of life since time immemorial, thereby conserving this national asset for you and the whole nation."[7]

As was remarked on several occasions:

"it would be naive to think that we can always find . . . common ground"[8]

"we are all devoted to the aims of our particular organisations and sometimes we get rather carried away with those"[9]

"they [tourism and conservation] have been in conflict from time immemorial, I should think."[10]

---

[1] Ev p 19.
[2] Ap 40 para 6.
[3] Q904.
[4] Q708.
[5] Q480.
[6] Mr Gordon Wordsworth (Ev not printed).
[7] Mr A R Cooper (Ev not printed).
[8] Q884.
[9] Q718.
[10] Q480.

29. Despite these sorts of cultural conflict, despite the public perception that the environment is under immediate threat from leisure use, and despite the potential of individual activities to spoil the natural heritage, however, we have found no evidence that leisure and tourism pose a serious, immediate or intrinsic threat to the environment. English Nature, who supplied us with the table of potential damage above, concluded overall that "Leisure activities do not in themselves represent the greatest threat to nature conservation."[1] In particular, leisure and tourism are less of a threat to Sites of Special Scientific Interest and Areas of Outstanding Natural Beauty than industry or other developments. According to English Nature's records, no Sites of Special Scientific Interest have been lost through tourist activity and most of any damage done is short- rather than long-term. Incidences of damage have decreased between 1989 and 1994; five cases of long-term damage to Sites of Special Scientific Interest by leisure use and fifty cases of short-term damage were reported in 1989/90 against four cases of long-term damage and 27 of short-term damage in 1993/94.

30. The Countryside Commission also noted that damage to the environment by industrialisation, farming and urbanisation "heavily exceeded" the damage caused by recreational activity.[2] These views were supported by, among others, the Ramblers' Association,[3] the Natural Environment Research Council[4] and New Forest District Council.[5]

31. Witnesses have also argued that leisure activities can have positive impacts on the countryside, in both economic terms and from the environmental viewpoint.[6] We were impressed by the Moors Valley Country Park in Dorset, which we visited when in the New Forest.[7] This was an example of a new Council-created family leisure facility on what was formerly poor agricultural land. It seemed to offer an enjoyable day out, especially for those with young children, and at the same time it had positively enhanced the local landscape.

32. **We note that according to the balance of evidence we received, compared to other activities, leisure and tourism do not cause significant widespread ecological damage to the countryside. However there is no need for complacency. We believe that there are important issues to address, involving transport, rural culture, and leisure management, as well as local conflicts in specific areas.**

33. **We also note that the cultural conflicts are just as real as, and sometimes more important than, the physical problems—indeed they are often the root cause of the various tensions and dissatisfactions that are redefined as threats to the environment.**

POTENTIAL IMPACTS OF SPECIFIC ACTIVITIES

Research

34. A number of witnesses referred to a lack of statistical evidence and research on the impact of tourism and leisure activities; and the non-existence of definitive visitor surveys.[8] In particular, it was put to us that activities such as jet-skiing and four-wheel drive use were being restricted on the basis of personal prejudice, in the absence of any data.

> "We need a very comprehensive range of research undertaken if we are to go from a point of knowledge rather than a point of opinion."[9]

> "People with their perceived views and entrenched opinions do not have documented evidence to back up their arguments for banning an activity and they are totally misleading and unfair to those who participate in the sports."[10]

---

[1] Ev p 105.
[2] Ev p 135.
[3] Ev p 234.
[4] Ap 40 para 8.
[5] Ev p 189.
[6] Business in Sport and Leisure pointed to this being achieved through sensitive development (Ev p 272), the Council for the Protection of Rural England through quiet and tranquil enjoyment of the countryside (Ev p 134).
[7] see Annex III.
[8] QQ436, 480, 511, 534, App 38, 42 para 2.5.5, 45.
[9] Q480.
[10] Ap 43.

35.   Those involved at the statutory level were more restrained in their assessment of the need for research. Bodies such as the Sports Council, the Countryside Commission, English Nature and the Departments of the Environment and National Heritage have budgets for commissioning research. The Department of the Environment referred us to some completed research, for example the Countryside Survey, but also pointed out some of the reasons why a comprehensive survey was so difficult to conduct, namely the variability of the effect of activities in different locations depending on the soil quality or the sensitivity of the environment.[1] This is also something that English Nature brought out in their evidence:

"Conducting research on things like the extent of disturbance on birds, for example, is extraordinarily difficult; there have been quite a number of projects over the last 15 years and, almost invariably, the results are inconclusive. There are so many different factors . . ."[2]

Dr Langslow, Chief Executive of English Nature stated "I do not think, from our point of view, there is a great deal of core research that we believe is essential."[3]

36.   The Sports Council pointed to the need for collaborative research between those agencies with responsibility for leisure and conservation. The Chief Executive, Mr Derek Casey, also told us that a meeting was planned "at chairman and chief executive level" to discuss this, among other issues.[4] Some of this collaboration is being co-ordinated by a group called the Countryside Recreation Network, from whom we received written evidence.[5] The Countryside Recreation Network summarise their remit as "exchanging and spreading information to develop best policy and practice in countryside recreation."[6] They also compile a directory of research.[7] Dr Langslow, Chief Executive of English Nature, confirmed their value to us:

"one of the values of the Countryside Recreation Network . . . is to try and identify what topics need to be done, and often provide a consortia of funding, because sometimes the scale of the projects are such that one agency does not feel it is important enough, but perhaps three together do feel that it is worth doing."[8]

37.   We commend new surveys which have been undertaken, such as the National Park Visitor Survey and the United Kingdom Day Visits Survey. **We feel that there is a need for further research to clarify national trends in recreational use, particularly in sport and active recreation in the countryside, which appear to have grown more rapidly than other activities in recent years. We commend the work of the Countryside Recreation Network in promoting research collaboration and suggest it reassess the priority given to work on environmental impacts, and places greater emphasis on developing a programme of work within the agencies to evaluate management initiatives. Given the difficulties in undertaking nationwide surveys of the ecological impact of leisure activities, we urge English Nature to continue to monitor those sites of greatest ecological sensitivity.**

Traffic

38.   The private car has given access to large areas of the countryside to large numbers of people, and brought with it a good deal of relaxation and pleasure. Ironically, however, the resulting cars, roads and car parks present a considerable threat to the quality of the landscape and environment that people set out to enjoy. Many witnesses picked out fumes, traffic congestion and parking problems as one of the worst environmental impacts of leisure activity.[9]

---

[1] Q31.
[2] Q333.
[3] *Ibid.*
[4] Q224.
[5] Ap 21.
[6] *Ibid.*
[7] *Ibid.*
[8] Q337.
[9] Ev pp 73, 136, Ap 50.

39. We received evidence that the use of the car for leisure purposes is becoming more significant.[1] This is shown by the table below.

TABLE 3

CAR TRAVEL	Journeys per person	Miles per person
1985/86	154	1,685
1991/93	179	2,200
Percentage change	+ 16 per cent	+ 31 per cent

However these figures cannot be extrapolated into trends in the recreational use of the countryside and this is a weakness of the present statistics. **We wish to see a reconciliation of the Countryside Commission's trend data, the United Kingdom Day Visitor Survey and the Department of Transport's statistics to produce an authoritative assessment of the use of the car for countryside recreation.**

Off-road vehicles and green lanes

40. Possible damage caused by vehicles driving 'off-road' was mentioned in the evidence we received, as can be seen from the summary table. Much of the concern seemed to be linked to established tracks known as 'green lanes.' In the Peak District we saw green lanes which were anything but green, suffering from a substantial amount of rutting which made them very difficult even for four-wheel drive vehicles to use. A substantial increase in the sale of four-wheel drive vehicles has occurred in recent years,[2] and has been blamed for the problem.[3] The Motoring Associations' Land Access and Recreation Association (LARA) suggested that most of the blame should be laid on the shoulders of highway authorities, who have failed to carry out their duty to maintain such routes. In particular, the failure to maintain drains causes serious problems.[4] There seems to be some substance to this view—certainly, it seemed that members of the Land Access and Recreation Association were doing more than some highway authorities to improve drainage. We commend the current negotiations in the Lake District which aim to involve the motoring organisations directly in maintenance work on the Garburn Road. This is an existing right of way which has been identified by the National Park Authority as one of a limited number of sustainable routes where off-road driving might be managed so as to be compatible with other uses.[5]

41. The issue has been complicated by the uncertain legal status of a number of such tracks, namely whether four-wheel drives have a right to use them. Part IV of the National Parks and Access to the Countryside Act 1949 imposed a duty on local authorities to survey and denote paths and lanes as a 'footpath', a 'bridleway' or a 'Road Used as Public Path'. Uncertainty developed about the last classification, therefore all Roads Used as Public Paths are to be reclassified either as Byways Open to All Traffic, which are, as the name implies, open to cars as well as horses, cycles and walkers, or as bridleways, which are not open to cars.

42. The reclassification was originally to be made on the basis of a test of "suitability"—"whether the way is suitable for vehicular traffic having regard to the position and width of the existing right of way, the condition and state of repair of the way, and the nature of the soil" as well as whether vehicular rights could be shown to exist.[6] However, problems arose with this process. Not only was it subjective, but reclassification of a Road Used as Public Path to a bridleway effectively removed vehicular rights on stretches of path where, in some cases, they could be shown to exist. The Wildlife and Countryside Act 1981 therefore removed the suitability test from reclassification. The process

---

[1] Leisure is for all purposes except travel to work, to school, on business, and shopping. It covers holidays, day trips, entertainment, sport and visiting friends. Source: DoE (National survey on travel for leisure purposes).
[2] Q744.
[3] Ev pp 74, 81.
[4] Q749.
[5] See Annex II.
[6] Countryside Act 1968.

now hinges on the demonstration of vehicular rights over history for a certain stretch of path. Several witnesses outlined their reasons for opposing the suitability test:

> "I think the suitability test was changed because it was seen quite clearly not to be working. What is suitable from one point of view is entirely unsuitable from another."[1]

43.   Others expressed the opposite view and argued for the re-introduction of the suitability test.[2]

44.   The new reclassification under the 1981 Act was to be done "as soon as reasonably practicable"[3] by the surveying authority. However, progress has been slow and varies between counties. The Countryside Commission, as part of its Year 2000 Rights of Way target,[4] has been attempting to encourage local authorities to get the legal definitions of such routes resolved. However, concerns and opposition to elements of the process have continued. Results from a 1990/91 survey suggest that 6,000km of Roads Used as Public Paths still exist in England and Wales.[5]

45.   The Country Landowners Association (CLA) were quite clear that the number of appeals had contributed to the delays.[6] The Rights of Way manager for Hampshire County Council stated in their evidence to us that there were other problems with the present tests:

> "The underlying problem is that a Road Used as Public Path may have become a Byway Open to All Traffic because of the historical use of the route by vehicles such as horse carts and not because of modern engine driven vehicles. While those involved in reclassification work understand this procedure it is impossible to justify to landowners and the public."[7]

46.   A historical use test may be legally convenient but it clearly creates problems for countryside managers, and all groups of potential users. Whilst a suitability test could be misused by local authorities, if it were subject to appeal procedures, it could assist highway authorities in negotiating access rights with four-wheel drive owners. We noted the large amount of evidence that the present system is not working. We believe that there is serious damage being done to Byways Open to All Traffic and Roads Used as Public Paths by their increasing use by four-wheel drive vehicles. We urge concerted action by Government and local highway authorities to discourage such damaging use of these rights of way.

47.   **We recommend that the Government carefully examine the mechanism contained in the Wildlife and Countryside Act 1981 whereby Roads Used as Public Paths (RUPPs) have to be reclassified as Byways Open to All Traffic (BOATs) if vehicular rights are shown to have ever existed. Instead, in consultation with all interested parties, they could be reclassified as bridleways or footpaths. We also suggest that 'Plain English' guides to this complicated procedure are produced and disseminated to the general public.**

Footpaths and Rights of Way

48.   Walking, as can be seen in the summary chart at the back of this Report, is one of the most popular countryside activities. Indeed, the National Farmers Union state that "we recognise that rights of way will remain at the core of recreational provision in the countryside."[8] Therefore we were particularly interested in issues relating to where, when and on what surface people may walk.

49.   The rights of way network is the principal means of visitor access to the countryside beyond the roads system, but, as the Edwards Report pointed out in 1991, its condition is not altogether satisfactory.[9] Some of the paths have become seriously eroded and, perhaps more seriously, others are inadequately waymarked, obstructed or overgrown. The Edwards Report recommended that National Park Authorities should provide an effective and accessible network of public rights of way, legally defined, properly waymarked and adequately maintained by 1995. **The Countryside Commission has endorsed the recommendation of the Edwards Report setting a target for all public rights of way in National Parks to be signposted where they leave the highway and to be**

---

[1] Q766.
[2] Q794.
[3] Wildlife and Countryside Act, 1981.
[4] Ev p 156.
[5] Source: Countryside Commission.
[6] Q875.
[7] Ev p 182.
[8] See Minutes of Evidence of 3 May (National Farmers Union memorandum).
[9] *Fit for the Future, Report of the National Parks Review Panel*, Countryside Commission, 1990.

free of all obstructions by the end of 1995, and everywhere by the year 2000. We believe these targets must be met. The Government should consider giving priority to the allocation of resources to the National Park Authorities to take on these responsibilities and encourage local authorities to meet their targets by the year 2000.

Watersports

50. Though there has been some public concern about the damage caused by watersports, we did not receive a great deal of evidence to back this up. We heard more evidence about such activities in the context of 'quiet enjoyment' in National Parks, particularly in the Lake District, where we discussed with those involved the proposal to ban craft travelling at speeds over 10mph on Lake Windermere, which at the time of writing was being considered by a Home Office Inspector after a Public Inquiry.[1]

51. The most common ill-effects noted by the National Rivers Authority (NRA) were visual impact and noise, damage to vegetation, trampling and litter. We also received some evidence relating to the use of jet-skis, especially during our site visits. Again summaries are found in the pull-out table. We would like to emphasise that it was put to us that one of the main problems about jet-skis was that such activities were not club based and therefore enforcement of good practice and the development of management schemes was proving difficult. These are matters we deal with later in this Report.[2]

52. Twenty years ago there were concerns about the effects of sub-aqua.[3] We received very little evidence of problems connected with this activity, and we hope that this means that good adherence to voluntary codes is being achieved in the sport. We also note that there have been concerns about pleasure boat activity, such as those expressed by the National Rivers Authority.[4] While acknowledging that any effects to the aquatic environment were more perceived than real, they expressed concern that new developments or the restoration of navigation could lead to more widespread problems. Overall, they concluded that "the impacts of [water- based] recreation on the environment are relatively minor and can be managed within the current organisational and legislative framework."[5]

53. In the context of wider concerns about ancillary development, English Nature expressed some concerns about marinas, which they stated led to habitat loss, particularly of mudflats and saltmarsh.[6] The British Marine Industries Federation stressed that "customers need the waterside provision of moorings, repair and storage in order to enjoy their boating. These boat yards are an integral part of the inland (river/canal/lake) and coastal/estuary shoreline scene." They recognised that "Each boating location needs to be considered on its individual merits with local circumstances often identifying the best management solution."[7] **If demand for marinas should arise in the future we feel efforts should be made to meet it by the development of redundant land (for example dockland) rather than using virgin riverbank or seashore.**

Angling

54. Of the eight activities the National Rivers Authority had researched, angling caused them most concern. Visual impact and noise, damage to vegetation, trampling and litter were reported as possible impacts as well as discarded tackle; the modification of fish species by means of fish stocking and the introduction of exotic species; and modifications to vegetation and habitat. There was also concern about bait-digging along the coast.[8] The relevant sporting associations repudiated many of these criticisms.[9] In particular, the National Federation of Sea Anglers drew attention to their "Bait Gatherers Code"[10] and on the matter of litter and discarded tackle, they outlined measures that they had imposed and reported a 95 per cent drop in the amount of discarded fishing line between 1979

---

[1] See Annex VI.
[2] See para 131.
[3] First Report from the Select Committee of the House of Lords on Sport and Leisure, Session 1972-73.
[4] Ap 38.
[5] *Ibid.*
[6] Ev p 107.
[7] British Marine Industries (Ev not printed).
[8] Ap 38.
[9] The National Federation of Anglers and the Salmon and Trout Association were both amused by complaints that the sport is intrusive (Ap 36, Salmon and Trout Association (Ev not printed)).
[10] Ap 46 para b.

and 1994.[1] The Salmon and Trout Association saw themselves as working to the same end as the National Rivers Authority; they expressed "extreme concern" about fish stocking and the introduction of exotic species, pointing out that regulations concerning the movement of freshwater fish are being "widely and continuously flouted." They also stated that they will support any National Rivers Authority measure to tighten up the regulations.[2]

Climbing

55.   We noted the possible impacts of climbing outlined in the evidence. These are summarised in the table at the back of this Report. We were pleased to learn of agreements between the British Mountaineering Council and bodies such as the Royal Society for the Protection of Birds which mean that climbs on certain cliffs are not used at nesting time. It would appear that these voluntary restrictions are largely respected, which reduces the disruptive potential of the sport.

56.   We were worried, though, by the potential threat of climbers moving on to more fragile types of rock, and the growth in the number of "rock gymnasts" who too often deface the cliffs by leaving permanent ironmongery behind. We were also extremely concerned by the call for the televising of the sport in the outdoors. Climbing makes exciting television, but whatever damage is done by pleasure climbers or "rock gymnasts" is multiplied as soon as camera crews, sound men and all the backup personnel of a major TV event arrive on the scene.[3] **We would strongly urge that any made-for-television competitive climbing events feature climbers using artificial rock walls rather than natural sites.**

Caving and Potholing

57.   We note that the impacts associated with this activity are seen as "limited" by English Nature, (they are listed in the table in the back of the Report) and we also note the admirable Code of Practice produced by the National Caving Association.[4] However **we felt the limits and conditions in the Code of Practice of the National Caving Association with regard to the use of mechanical excavators, the construction of dams, diversions of water courses and the use of explosives[5] are too weak.**

Golf

58.   In their document "Leisure Landscapes"[6] the Council for the Protection of Rural England documents a rapid expansion in the use of rural land for golf courses, and outlines the damage it believes golf courses cause to the natural landscape and ecology. The Council for the Protection of Rural England expressed concerns that although the boom in the construction of golf courses has been temporarily halted, expansion will resume "as the economy picks up." Golf courses were also identified as causes for concern by English Nature.[7] We note that discussion between the English Golf Union and the Ramblers' Association has ironed out many of the problems with footpaths and rights of way. **We commend the Code of Practice for golf courses designed by English Nature, which we hope will encourage better design and maintenance, and a more natural use of the land.[8]** The controversy over golf courses arose in the Cotswold Area of Outstanding Natural Beauty (fewer areas more sensitive) before they were built. Once completed the controversy subsided and indeed it could be argued that they create a better wildlife habitat than intensively farmed agricultural land. **We recommend that any future proposals for golf courses be subjected to more detailed environmental assessment and scrutiny by planning authorities in order to minimise their impact on sensitive landscapes, to create new wildlife habitats and to improve public access.**

---

[1] Ap 37.
[2] Salmon and Trout Association (Ev not printed).
[3] See Annex II.
[4] Ap 35.
[5] Ap 35 para 1.4.3.
[6] *Leisure Landscapes: Leisure, Culture and the English Countryside, Challenges and Conflicts*, CPRE, May 1994.
[7] Ev p 1.
[8] Ap 25.

OTHER ISSUES

Access

59.   We believe that the opening up of additional areas of the countryside to public access would have advantages: it would help to reduce pressure on "honeypot" sites, give people new environments to enjoy, and enhance visitor knowledge of, and willingness to contribute to, the protection of the natural landscape. However, opening up the countryside to visitors is not without controversy. Arguments put to us by the Ramblers' Association and the National Farmers' Union typified the positions which might be adopted. On the one hand, the Ramblers' Association, believing that the countryside is a common heritage, has argued for a "right to roam" on all uncultivated land (on mountain, heath, moorland and woodland and along the seashore). On the other hand, the National Farmers' Union, stressing that "the farm is a workplace", has been concerned about the "inappropriate use" of the countryside.[1] This difference of opinion was mirrored in the Committee.

60.   One possible way of resolving these differences is by the sort of compromise reached in the National Parks and Access to the Countryside Act 1949. The Act gave National Parks and local authorities powers to negotiate and pay landowners and farmers for access agreements.[2] Though many have not shown much enthusiasm for this approach, the Peak District National Park is a prime example of its successful operation. Although delays have occurred in the renegotiation of some of the agreements, they have been outstandingly successful in achieving public access to much of the Peak District.[3]

61.   More recently the Countryside Commission has included access provision within the Countryside Stewardship Scheme. As a result, 13,517 hectares of open land and 3970 km of footpaths are now open to the public.[4] However, the Ramblers' Association has been critical of the scheme, arguing that the £8 million to be spent on it over the next ten years is not good value for money and pointing out that many of the areas covered by it are not well signed and are not themselves of high landscape value.[5] We believe that this can be remedied when the scheme is transferred from the Countryside Commission to the Ministry of Agriculture, Fisheries and Food. It ought then to be possible to expand and improve the access elements. The same is true for land exempted from inheritance tax in return for access: the access so provided must be made known to the public at large.

62.   **We feel that access agreements can contribute to resolving the conflicting interests of walkers, farmers and landowners. We urge the National Parks Authorities, local authorities and the Ministry of Agriculture, Fisheries and Food to pursue access agreements with vigour. We believe that access should be significantly increased by the year 2000.**

Development of Leisure Facilities

63.   English Nature stated in their evidence to the Committee that with regard to leisure and tourism, "impacts from associated development often represent a greater threat"[6] including "the loss of habitat and species" and "demand for improved and enlarged facilities and infrastructure including roads." They listed marinas, golf courses and caravan parks as examples of such development.[7] The Natural Environment Research Council similarly noted "The bigger loss/fragmentation/disturbance of habitats [compared to the impact of the actual activities] will come from the building of infrastructure such as roads to provide better access."[8] We note these concerns and deal with issues of development later in this Report when we consider the planning system.[9]

---

[1]   See Minutes of evidence of 3 May,(National Farmers Union memorandum).
[2]   The following number of access agreements have been made by National Parks under the National Parks and Access to the Countryside Act 1949: Dartmoor 1, Exmoor 0, Lake District 24, Northumberland 2, North York Moors 0, Peak Park 20, Yorkshire Dales 1. A number have also been made under the Wildlife and Countryside Act 1981, for example Dartmoor National Park Authority make a much larger number of management and access agreements under both Acts.
[3]   See Minutes of Evidence of 10 May (Department of the Environment supplementary memorandum).
[4]   Source: Countryside Commission.
[5]   *Countryside Stewardship Scheme: Public Access Sites, A Report into the value for money and effectiveness of purchasing public access to the countryside via a government-funded experimental scheme*, Ramblers Association, March 1995.
[6]   Ev p 105.
[7]   Ev p 107.
[8]   Ap 40.
[9]   See para 87.

Loss of Local Character

64.   A substantial part of the Report by the Council for the Protection of Rural England, 'Leisure Landscapes', was concerned with the cultural impacts of tourism and day-tripping on 'host communities.' They suggested that there could be two possible impacts; firstly that promotion of 'heritage Britain' and some of its practical manifestations, for example standard white-on-brown signs, acted to reduce local diversity and somehow developed the worst and most stereotypical brand of 'Olde England';[1] and secondly that leisure development often used "poor and sub-standard design and inappropriate materials."[2] The Department of the Environment evidence did not address this issue head-on but referred to examples of 'good practice' such as the National Trust which they stated "can demonstrate an extensive record of site management, providing for access while maintaining reasonable safeguards to protect the landscape."[3] **We recommend that design standards for leisure development should be strictly enforced through the planning system to ensure that development is of an appropriate form and material for the local environment.**

Impact on local communities

65.   The National Farmers' Union listed in their evidence aspects of inconvenience to farmers which could be caused by leisure activities "if visitors choose not to respect the farm as a workplace."[4] We heard further evidence of possible conflicts between visitors and local people when on our visits.[5] In general, the disadvantages of leisure and tourism to those who work and live in the countryside include traffic,[6] footpath wear resulting in mud and rutting,[7] loss of privacy and peace, loss of local amenities (for example, through the replacement of grocers' shops with tourist shops)[8] and litter.

66.   Residents of villages near the Cotswold Water Park, which we visited,[9] voiced concerns about the "cumulative impact of piecemeal development."[10] While acknowledging possible economic benefits, they stated that "Leisure development...must be sympathetic to the settlements and the people living there."[11]

67.   The positive impacts of tourism on rural areas include employment and support for local services. The Rural Development Commission stated that tourism is worth £8bn a year to England's rural areas, generating 400,000 jobs.[12] Around one-fifth of all overnight stays and almost one in three of all day trips by United Kingdom residents are spent in the countryside. It is estimated that these generate associated expenditure of approximately £2.3 billion a year.[13] At the local level, the bulk of the economic and associated benefits come from visitors who stay overnight.[14] Over 30 per cent of holiday expenditure is on accommodation.[15]

68.   A Report on the economic impacts of the Center Parcs developments in Sherwood and Elveden by the Rural Development Commission concluded that the additional incomes and visitors' expenditure amounted to £4.5m in the local area round Sherwood and £5.3m round Elveden. This accounted for a total of between 980 and 1109 jobs each year when the Parcs were operating.[16] The Report concluded that "The benefits are substantial in terms of incomes and jobs."[17]

69.   The Rural Development Commission is at present preparing a Report on the indirect benefits of tourism to rural areas, for example extra bus services and survival of village shops, which is to be published in September 1995. The Department of the Environment stated to us that "in some rural

---

[1] White-on-brown signs are part of the national system of road signing which is uniform throughout the country and based on principles of safety and ease of recognition for the user. There are currently proposals to allow a more relaxed attitude to the use of brown signs which is causing some concern to the Region Tourist Boards.
[2] Ev p 135.
[3] Ev p 12.
[4] See Minutes of Evidence of 3 May (National Farmers Union memorandum).
[5] See Annexes II to VI.
[6] See para 143.
[7] See para 116.
[8] See Annex III.
[9] See Annex V.
[10] Ap 18.
[11] *Ibid.*
[12] Ap 47.
[13] *Ibid.*
[14] Q505.
[15] *Tourism: Competing with the Best,* DNH, 1995.
[16] *The Economic Impact of Holiday Villages,* Rural Development Commission, 1991.
[17] *Ibid.*

communities tourism and leisure activities may make the difference between closure and viability for shops, pubs and other vital services"[1] **We feel that it is important that the positive economic impacts of leisure and tourism on rural areas are recognised.**

CONCLUSION

70.   In conclusion, the evidence given to us in both written and oral form shows that the central question is not whether tourism and leisure activities are damaging to the environment, but how conflicts about land-use can be resolved. These conflicts include practical disputes between incompatible user-groups about what are, or are not, "suitable" country activities; aesthetic arguments; cultural conflicts; economic disputes between different groups of country dwellers; and conflicts caused by the exacerbation of pre-existing problems such as access, traffic and pollution.

71.   **We see no immediate need to impose any general restrictions on leisure activities in order to provide blanket protection for the rural environment.** We believe the general approach to ensuring that any harmful environmental impacts of leisure are mitigated is by planning and management and this is the subject of the following sections of this Report.

PLANNING AND MANAGING TOURISM AND LEISURE

72.   As the impacts of leisure and tourism on the environment are diverse, so are the official bodies which deal with them, as the box below shows:

Government Departments:
    Department of the Environment
    Department of National Heritage

    —

    Department of Health
    Department of Transport
    Forestry Commission
    Ministry of Agriculture, Fisheries and Food

Statutory Bodies sponsored by the Department of the Environment:
    British Waterways Board
    Countryside Commission
    English Nature
    National Rivers Authority
    Rural Development Commission

Statutory Bodies sponsored by the Department of National Heritage:
    British Tourist Authority
    English Tourist Board
    Sports Council

Regional Bodies:
    Regional Councils for Sport and Recreation
    Regional Tourist Boards

    —

    National Park Authorities
    Local Authorities

We explain their relative responsibilities, relevant area designations and legislation in Annex I of this Report.

THE PUBLIC SECTOR

Government Departments

73.   The promotion of tourism and leisure and the mitigation of their effects on the environment form an important part of the work of a number of government departments and agencies. We summarise their roles and responsibilities in an Annex. Considering the number of different agencies involved, we sought to examine how policy on leisure and the environment is being co-ordinated.

[1] Ev p 3.

74.   We shared some of the concerns of bodies such as the Council for the Protection of Rural England[1] and Business in Sport and Leisure[2] about the level of co-ordination between the Department of National Heritage and the Department of the Environment. As the tourism industry is extremely fragmented[3], any policy must be clear if it is to be effective. We expected the Department of National Heritage to be taking the lead in co-ordinating the leisure-related responsibilities of other Departments and publicising their work through its tourism publications. The Department of National Heritage, however, stated that they viewed their objectives as being primarily economic, and reflected this in their publications and policy line. Promotion of good environmental practice was delegated to the English Tourist Board.[4]

75.   **We recommend that the Department of National Heritage assume a more pro-active role in developing tourism and leisure policies taking into account issues of the environment, rural transport and agriculture. The Department should ensure that the content of its publications reflects this role.**

Tourism Task Force

76.   In 1990, the then sponsoring Department for tourism, the Department of Employment, set up the 'Tourism Task Force' in response to public interest in the future of the environment and growing concerns about the sheer "weight of visitors" to certain historic towns, heritage sites and sensitive parts of the countryside.[5] The Task Force brought together representatives of tourism and environmental interests from the public and private sectors, and from national and local government. The Task Force's Report, 'Tourism and the Environment: Maintaining the Balance' was published in May 1991 and gave examples of good practice, as well as discussing the possible problems caused by large numbers of visitors to sensitive sites.

Statutory Bodies

77.   The Countryside Commission's memorandum suggested that we should take an interest in the roles of the different government agencies, saying that:

> "There is a need for relevant government agencies to be able to act in a brokering role between different interests in a positive and fair way to achieve consensus for action. The Committee needs to reaffirm the value of these inputs, as some are under threat of partial or total withdrawal."[6]

It was explained that this included concerns about the roles both of the English Tourist Board and the Sports Council.

English Tourist Board

78.   Witnesses from the Countryside Commission agreed with those from the English Tourist Board (ETB) that funding cuts affected the English Tourist Board's future role in researching and ameliorating the environmental impacts of leisure activities.'[7] As the English Tourist Board has been most closely involved in promoting environmental good practice to the tourism industry, this is of some concern to us. **We trust that the Department of National Heritage will ensure that the English Tourist Board's work in promoting environmental good practice to the tourism industry will continue. We note that at present the Board is undertaking a five-year evaluation of the "effect of its interventions in the market."[8] This should include analysis of its effectiveness in promoting good environmental practice.**

[1] QQ394-5.
[2] Q808.
[3] Q84.
[4] *Ibid.*
[5] *Tourism and the Environment : Maintaining the Balance*, English Tourist Board and the Employment Department Group, May 1991.
[6] Ev p 152.
[7] Departmental expenditure on the Board was £16.2 million in 1992/93; it is expected to fall to £11.3 million in 1994/95 and £10.0 million each in 1995/96 and 1996/97. The Department of National Heritage pointed out in their 1994 Annual Report that the non-Government funding to the English Tourist Board in 1992/93 had increased 15 per cent compared to the previous year.
[8] Department of National Heritage Annual Report 1994.

Sports Council

79.   Professor Allan Patmore, a Countryside Commissioner, voiced concerns to us about proposals to restructure and refocus the Sports Council:

> "it grieves me to see them move out of the very area that has always attracted me most and I think has meant most to the greatest number of people, which is the countryside area."[1]

80.   He also voiced concerns about the funding implications of the proposals[2] at a time when the Countryside Commission's budget for recreation was set to decrease from £6.5 million in 1995/96 to £6.2 million in 1997/98.[3] For this and other reasons, the Countryside Commission could not step into the 'gap' which they expected to appear:

> "whether or not we can simply step into that work, I think the answer has to be no; it is a very reluctant no . . . It is primarily resources, but it is also remit. Ours is the much greater area of access to the countryside as a whole. The Sports Council was concerned in particular with links with the governing bodies of sport, we do not have that kind of tradition."[4]

81.   We recognise that there is some uncertainty about the Sports Council restructuring and the effects it will have on other Government bodies, not least among those bodies themselves. We feel that it is unfortunate that the Sports Council is moving away from its remit to promote informal recreation in the countryside, considering the links which exist between it and the governing bodies of sport. Action is necessary to ensure that the bodies which may have to assume extra responsibilities in the area are able to do such preparatory work as is necessary.

82.   **We recommend that the Department of the Environment, Department of National Heritage, English Tourist Board, Sports Council and Countryside Commission issue a clear and specific joint statement of their relative roles and responsibilities towards leisure and tourism in the countryside. This could be part of the documentation produced in association with the Sports Council's restructuring.**

83.   Where responsibility for policy implementation is being distributed between a number of statutory bodies, the importance of co-ordination between them cannot be overstated. There are examples where such co-ordination has taken place, such as in the production by the Sports Council and the Countryside Commission of 'Good Practice in the Planning and Management of Active Recreation in the Countryside' in April 1995. The continuance of such initiatives is the responsibility of sponsoring government departments.

National Parks

84.   We welcome the Government's provision for National Parks in the Environment Bill. We believe that their new status will help them to play an even more effective part in managing the countryside. However, as the Peak Park Joint Planning Board represented to us so strongly, they can only take on an enhanced role if they have the financial resources to carry out their responsibilities.[5]

85.   We were impressed by the warden/ranger service when on our visits to the Lake and Peak Districts. The full-time and part-time wardens are supplemented by volunteers. We would like to take this opportunity to pay tribute to all the work they do. Many National Parks are making use of conservation volunteers in one form or another, and all this voluntary effort makes an important contribution to the maintenance of our National Parks. It should, however, be seen as an extra resource and never an excuse for underfunding.

86.   **In many ways the work of the National Park Authorities epitomises the management approach that we are advocating. We would like to see this approach extended to other well-used areas of the English countryside. But good management and good conservation are expensive. We believe that funding for these authorities should allow for the necessary investment in good practice which is sustainable and which is in keeping with local scale and needs within available resources.**

---

[1] Q405.
[2] Q406.
[3] *Ibid.*
[4] QQ405-406.
[5] Q237.

GUIDANCE AND PRINCIPLES

Policy Planning and Guidance

87.   The chosen method for resolving environmental conflicts has traditionally been the planning system, though some of the issues related to leisure and tourism are not covered by it. National planning priorities are set out in Planning Policy and Guidance (PPG) notes, of which a number are relevant to leisure in the countryside:

PPG 2: Green Belts   PPG 7: The Countryside and the Rural Economy
PPG 9: Nature Conservation   PPG 13: Transport
PPG 17: Sport and Recreation   PPG 20: Planning the Coast
PPG 21 Tourism

88.   We received an interesting variety of opinions with regard to this policy guidance. Business in Sport and Leisure, representing private sector leisure companies, commented that "The current PPGS and circulars do not adequately accommodate the needs of the industry in many ways, but give ample exhortation to ensure protection of the environment." [1] The Countryside Commission said the planning system as a whole worked well, but believed that PPG 17 would benefit from being reviewed and updated "in the light of more recent developments in the concept of sustainability."[2] This was also appoint raised by the Council for the Protection of Rural England. [3]

89.   The Royal Town Planning Institute recommended that PPG 21 should be revised to include consideration of the effects on the countryside from people and their means of transport, and that it should deal with 'Green Tourism'.[4] They also stated that PPGs 13, 20 and 21 should be rewritten to take more account of the pressures and impacts on the environment from leisure traffic.[5] The Association of County Councils listed in their memorandum[6] some suggested changes to the planning guidance in National Parks, which included:

— a more forthright statement of the need to exercise restraint in granting permission for signs and outdoor advertisements (PPG 19 - Outdoor Advertisement Control);[7] and

— not attempting to encourage visits to the Parks during the quiet winter period (through PPG 21).

90.   We note these suggestions. **There has been no common call for major changes in the national Planning Policy Guidance. We feel that an update of PPG 17 to bring it into line with the concept of sustainability is desirable, and we request that this issue and the comments quoted in this Report be addressed by the Department of the Environment in their response to us.**

Regional Planning Guidance

91.   There is also a regional element to the planning system. The Department of the Environment issues Regional Planning Guidance (RPG) which cover "matters requiring consideration on a wider geographical basis than that of individual county structure plans."[8] Local authorities have an input into the regional planning process. The finished Regional Planning Guidance notes are to be taken account of by local authorities alongside national Planning Policy Guidance notes, as the Secretary of State's guidance which specifically addresses regional issues. More informal regional strategies come from the Regional Councils for Sport and Recreation and the regional tourist boards.

Regional Councils for Sport and Recreation

92.   There are 10 Regional Councils for Sport and Recreation (RCSRs) in England.[9] They are non-statutory bodies which bring together representatives from the public and voluntary sectors at various times during the year to discuss issues related to recreation and sport. They are listed as

[1] Ev p 275.
[2] Ev p 156.
[3] Ev p 139.
[4] See Minutes of Evidence of 3 May (Royal Town Planning Institute memorandum para 27).
[5] *Ibid.*
[6] Ev p 256.
[7] See para 64.
[8] DoE Annual Report 1994.
[9] Northern Region, Yorkshire and Humberside Region, North West Region, West Midlands Region, East Midlands Region, Eastern Region, Greater London Region, South East Region, Southern Region, South Western Region.

consultees for the preparation of Regional Planning Guidance notes[1] and also regarding issues related to the General Development Order which would lead to the loss of sports facilities.[2]

93.   Much concern has arisen from the announcement that after the Sports Council's restructuring[3] the Regional Councils for Sport and Recreation will have to provide their own secretariat (at the moment the regional offices of the Sports Council perform this function). Witnesses from the Countryside Commission called on the Government to safeguard the Councils' future; Business in Sport and Leisure suggested that the Regional Councils for Sport and Recreation often provide the only strategic forum for discussing sport and recreation at a regional level.[4] They also suggested that private sector membership of the Regional Councils for Sport and Recreation would be a useful development.[5]

94.   **We recommend that the Department of National Heritage assume responsibility for ensuring that the removal of the Sports Council secretariat does not result in the disappearance of the Regional Councils for Sport and Recreation or lead to a deterioration in their effectiveness.**

Strategic Regional Provision for "difficult" sports

95.   PPG 17 (Sport and Recreation) sets out where responsibility should lie for various areas of planning for leisure and sport:

Regional Planning Guidance	County Structure Plans
Contains policies for particular major facilities or centres which are of regional, national or international importance; contains policies for natural landscape features and wildlife habitats having potential for recreation (eg mountains, woodlands, rivers, estuaries, coastline), where there may be a conflict of priorities; contains policies for the urban fringe, large areas of open land within conurbations, the countryside and Green Belts; and sets out implications for sport and recreation provision of strategic policies for new development	Identify the scope for major sport and recreation initiatives (eg community forests, use of redundant mineral sites); provide guidance on sport and recreation provision affecting all or significant parts of the country; and offer strategic guidance on other issues needing countrywide policies such as the protection of sensitive areas from inappropriate sport and recreation, and the provision of football stadia and other major facilities

96.   We have sympathy with the views expressed by some of the sporting organisations; for example, their recommendations that planning guidance should recognise:

— the principle of "fair access for all rather than . . . further legislation which will penalise legitimate sport and recreation."[6]

— the argument that it is better to make adequate provision for leisure uses rather than to encourage uncontrolled use by the imposition of restrictions[7]

— the view that excessive restriction on new development can lead to undue pressure on existing facilities.[8]

97.   We are worried that certain activities perceived as "nuisances"— water-skiing for example, are denied facilities and hounded from area to area. The British Water Ski Federation, in a supplementary memorandum, was able to document the way that recent local planning decisions excluded water-skiers from sites they had previously used, in most cases without offering them

---

[1] PPG 17 (Sport and Recreation).
[2] DoE Circular 9/95; General Development Order Consolidation 1995; Table 2, page 28.
[3] See para 79.
[4] Ev p 275.
[5] Q805.
[6] Ap 1.
[7] *Ibid.*
[8] See Minutes of Evidence of 3 May (Royal Town Planning Institute memorandum para 20).

alternatives.[1] Northumberland County Council, for example, told the Federation in March 1995 that they intended to exclude water-skiiers from Ladyburn Lake one day per weekend on the grounds that water-skiing "is considered a deterrent to other groups" and that in general it is "incompatible with their aim of widening participation in watersports."[2] Similarly, the Draft Norfolk Broads Plan of 1993 stated that "The Broads Authority views water-skiing as an inappropriate use of the Broads" and was "considering a date by which time it should be removed from the waterways." Its promise to "examine opportunities for alternative sites" was so worded that it did not sound encouraging. [3] Attempts to drive out such activities, site by site and area by area, are likely to lead to continuing conflicts, an increase in the number of controversial public inquiries such as at Windermere, and increasing and unplanned pressure on those sites which have not yet been restricted but which may in turn come under pressure for restrictions.

98.   The desire to protect sensitive areas from intrusive activities is understandable. But this can only be achieved in the long run through regional planning strategies which encourage into use, or into more intensive use, less sensitive sites.

99.   On small bodies of water, and in particular in areas of the country where water sites are scarce, pressures will have to be lifted by providing extra sites. **We recommend that new, appropriate sites should be sought for watersports, particularly power-boating, water-skiing and jet-skiing. These sites should be developed close to large urban centres so as to reduce leisure travel with its attendant fumes and congestion.**

100.   This development of 'positive provision' for noisy and unpopular activities should not be restricted to watersports. **We would like to see much more emphasis put on positive planning.** We note the views of the Country Landowners Association, who stated in their recent submission to the Government's consultation on the Rural White Paper that "a constant criticism from Country Landowners Association membership is that the Development Plan system fails to deliver the Government's policy through, first of all, inadequate policies in development plans and, ultimately, a negative Development Control process."[4]

101.   At local level we believe that local development plans must help to meet regional needs for all leisure, recreational and sporting activities, and should actively consider matters relating to landscape, amenity and nature conservation.

102.   **We also urge planners to recognise that the principle of sustainability in leisure and recreation involves the provision of facilities for all activities, not only for the aesthetically pleasing and non-intrusive ones. We believe that this might be best achieved at regional level without damaging the environment or increasing conflicts between different user groups by identifying sites suitable for noisy and obtrusive activities. Derelict land or land of low amenity value might be developed for leisure use, reducing pressure on existing facilities and to some extent segregating incompatible sporting activities.**

103.   We note efforts which have been made to develop and use technology to decrease the impacts of such activities, for example the use of quieter electric motors.[5]

104.   **It would obviously aid their case if manufacturers of leisure equipment, such as power-boats, jet-skis, trail bikes, and so on were to develop quieter motors to minimise disturbance and noise pollution. Efforts should be made to reduce engine noise at the point of manufacture; we would suggest that noise is often a question of image rather than necessity. Organisers of clay pigeon shoots and other "difficult" events have a similar responsibility to recognise the offence their activities cause to others, and to take realistic and effective steps to reduce the disturbance they cause.**

105.   Some activities and events which are undoubtedly 'noisy' have taken place in the same area for many years. We would press National Park Authorities to have regard for such traditions when restricting them. If it is felt that the activity should be curtailed in a particular locality, efforts should be made to provide for it somewhere else. **We recommend that planning strategies should identify clearly both sites where intrusive activities are to be restricted and sites where such activities are to be permitted or encouraged. We urge the Government to issue appropriate guidance to local authorities on the preparation of structure plans.**

---

[1] British Water Ski Federation supplementary evidence (not printed).
[2] *Ibid.*
[3] *Ibid.*
[4] *Towards a Rural Policy. A vision for the Twenty-First Century*, County Landowners Association, 1995.
[5] See Annex V.

PLANNING FOR SPECIFIC LANDSCAPES

Coasts

106.   The measures we suggest in this Report are equally applicable to rural and coastal areas. We discussed issues particularly related to the coast on our visit to Studland and Poole Harbour.[1] We received evidence on various planning issues of particular relevance to the Coastal Zone, some of which related to recommendations made by our predecessor Committee in the 1987-92 Parliament.

107.   Their Report on Coastal Zone Protection and Planning was published on 28 April 1992,[2] and the Government responded the following July.[3] The conclusions and recommendations pointed to the need for an integrated approach to the planning and management of the coast. To achieve this aim, the Committee recommended the treatment of inshore waters, intertidal areas and maritime land as one integrated "Coastal Zone". In practice, it suggested: the development of a National Coastal Strategy by Government; the review of options and consultation concerning the establishment of a National Coastal Zone Unit; and the development of Coastal Zone Management Plans and Groups based on natural coastal "cells."

108.   In October 1993 the Department of the Environment and Welsh Office published 'Managing the Coast: a Review of Coastal Management Plans in England and Wales and the Powers Supporting Them', and 'Development Below Low Water Mark: a Review of Regulation in England and Wales.' Both consultation documents were intended as responses to recommendations made in the Committee's Report. The Ministry of Agriculture, Fisheries and Food also issued consultation and then final policy documents on coastal and flood defence and shoreline management plans.

109.   This Committee held a follow-up evidence session on 16 March 1994 with officials from the Department of the Environment and the Ministry of Agriculture, Fisheries and Food to discuss the documents and the Committee's continuing concerns about coastal policy. Subsequently, on 15 July 1994, the Department of the Environment announced a number of new initiatives in coastal planning: a statement of policy guidelines for the coast; a standing forum on coastal zone management; action to highlight good practice on coastal zone management plans; and a review of by-law powers relating to coastal management. It was also announced that a statement of national policy guidelines for the coast would be produced 'within the year.' The first meeting of the standing forum (the 'Coastal Forum') whose purpose is to "provide a vehicle for discussion of broad issues at the national level" took place on 13 December 1994. More recent developments have included the announcement by the Department of the Environment on 5 May 1995 that it had commissioned a consortium to produce a guide "highlighting best practice for bodies preparing coastal management plans." The Ministry of Agriculture, Fisheries and Food also launched "Shoreline Management Plans"—new guidance for coastal defence authorities which "stressed the virtues of strategic planning and local consultation" on 5 June 1995.

110.   The evidence we received pointed out that these factors had implications for leisure in the Coastal Zone. [4] In particular, the frequent lack of jurisdiction of planning authorities in areas below the low water mark was pointed out as reason to encourage management plans in such areas.[5]

111.   **In relation to planning policies in the Coastal Zone, we endorse the findings of our predecessors. We believe that progress in this area, while it is to be welcomed, is still too slow.**

Forests

112.   We published a Report in the 1992-93 Session on 'Forestry and the Environment,'[6] which pressed the Government to develop a more synthesised approach to forestry policy. Recommendations pointed toward the need for clearer lines of Ministerial responsibility and the need for a national strategy "umbrella" which would also set out priorities for achieving set objectives in different forests and different situations. We suggested that one way to achieve some of these objectives would be the development of a United Kingdom forestry strategy, accompanied by policy statements for England,

[1]   See Annex III.
[2]   Second Report from the Environment Committee, HC(1991-92)17.
[3]   *Managing the Coast: a Review of Coastal Management Plans in England and Wales and the Powers Supporting Them; and Development Below Low Water Mark: a Review of Regulation in England and Wales,* Cm 2011.
[4]   Ev p 233, Ap 26.
[5]   See Minutes of Evidence of 3 May (Royal Town Planning Institute memorandum, para 17).
[6]   First Report from the Environment Committee HC(1992-93)257.

Wales, Scotland and Northern Ireland. We also supported the principles behind multi-purpose forestry, and recommended that these be adopted in the development and management of the Community and National Forests.

113.   Since then, there have been several recent developments in policy and practice. The Government published a Command Paper entitled 'Our Forests: the Way Ahead' in August 1994.[1] This proposed that a Next Steps Agency 'Forest Enterprise' be set up to manage the Forestry Commission woodlands, and made other proposals relating to management, including the introduction of incentives to improve management and timber production, and the encouragement of public access. However, no strategy as suggested above has been completed, and other of our concerns remain unaddressed.

114.   We considered issues relating to leisure in forest areas when on our visit to the New Forest.[2] The Forestry Commission submitted evidence to us outlining their measures to encourage private owners to provide woodland access through their Woodland Grant Scheme,[3] and their own policy of "encouraging recreational use wherever this is feasible."[4] They also outlined their policy of catering for "a wide number of specialist sports and activities,"[5] based on the assumption that "woodland can provide a location for sports that, in open areas, might be noisy or obtrusive."[6] This policy has been opposed by some local groups.[7] **We note the need to keep forest policy and the impacts of leisure activities upon it under review.** We also recognise the importance of small scale education and training projects which woodland areas can offer.

Footpaths

115.   The largest proportion of the rights of way network is made up of footpaths. Some are problematical: many were never recorded on the definitive maps, a few were recorded inaccurately and the legal status of a few is complex. Though we can accept that some of these problems may take a little longer to resolve, we hope the majority can be resolved by the year 2000.

Erosion

116.   The largest single footpath issue about which we received evidence was erosion, particularly in upland regions.[8] Some eroded paths are extremely unsightly, some were almost impassable and in a few cases the erosion was spreading outwards over a very wide area.[9] According to the evidence we were given, the causes are complex. Contributing factors are: high stock levels on the land crossed;[10] frequency of use, particularly in bad weather;[11] bad drainage of the path and surrounding land;[12] and the nature of path surfaces.[13] We saw various solutions in operation. We regret to say that some of them appear inappropriate or ineffective. Some only lead to worse erosion a few years later. In other cases, very substantial physical work has been undertaken which has changed the nature of the path from hillside track to a paved way not unlike an urban footpath. In these cases, the cure is worse than the disease. We believe that ineffective work and overkill must both be avoided.

117.   **We believe that footpath work should be subject to a consistent Code of Practice. We endorse the Code produced by a Joint Working Group of the Lake District National Park Authority, English Nature and the National Trust:**

"The repair and maintenance of paths in open country will be subject to the following considerations:

   (a) That the repairs are necessary to prevent or ameliorate visual intrusion and environmental damage;

[1] Cm 2644.
[2] See Annex III.
[3] Ev p 171.
[4] *Ibid.*
[5] *Ibid.*
[6] *Ibid.*
[7] Ap 49.
[8] Ap 20 para 5.
[9] See Annexes II and VI.
[10] Ap 49.
[11] Ev p 74.
[12] Ap 49.
[13] Ev p 72, Ap 49.

(b) **Works should be of a high standard of design and implementation using indigenous materials, sympathetic in colour and texture to the immediate surrounding area. Uniformity of construction should be avoided, e.g. steps;**

(c) **Techniques used should protect existing vegetation and, normally, only locally occurring plant species should be used in restoration. Non-local species will be acceptable only where necessary as a 'nurse crop', and where natural succession will rapidly result in their disappearance;**

(d) **The more remote the path, the more stringently the criteria for path repairs should be applied. This will be a matter of judgement but, in general, the more remote or wild the location, the less acceptable an obviously engineered path will be;**

(e) **Repaired paths should be suitable to the routes used and constructed on a scale appropriate for the intended use as a footpath, bridleway or byway; and**

(f) **Before any repair work is agreed, the question should be asked 'is there a better solution?'**

The use of waymarks, cairns or other intrusive features, other than those traditionally established on summits and path junctions, will be discouraged.

A sustained commitment of resources to path management will be sought, so that small scale continuous maintenance can replace infrequent major repairs as the normal method of path management."[1]

118.   **We also welcome the efforts of the British Upland Footpath Trust[2] to provide funds for the sensitive restoration of upland footpaths.**

119.   We were particularly concerned about the problems being experienced on national long-distance footpaths and other trails. Neither Tom Stevenson, in campaigning for the Pennine Way, nor A.R. Wainwright in promoting the coast to coast path, could have envisaged how popular such routes would become or what problems would be caused by that popularity. Owing to the fragile nature of many path surfaces, some sections of these routes have not been able to cope with the high levels of use they have been subjected to. Restoration of the Pennine Way, for example, has been estimated to cost £7 million and ongoing maintenance will require £750,000 each year.'[3] Considering the natural tendency of peat to erode and turn to bog, and the fact that walkers are quite capable of finding alternative routes, thus easing pressure on affected sections; considering too that the repairs can be more unsightly and unnatural than the "damage"; we feel that a policy of carrying out extensive resurfacing work on such routes must be reconsidered.

120.   We also feel that if existing trails are promoted by individuals or bodies such as local authorities, or if new ones are designated in the future, it is essential that they follow naturally sustainable routes or that a wide variety of alternative routes should be provided to disperse visitors, rather than pouring money into unsustainable paths and defacing the landscape with unnatural tracks. **We hope that the Countryside Commission's consultation on the maintenance of National Trails will allow re-routing, temporary diversions, and the provision of alternative lines of route.**

Dogs

121.   One particular footpath problem involves dogs. At Studland Bay, for example, the right of way runs along the shore. The National Trust told us that dogs cannot therefore be banned from the beach, and that getting a poop-scoop scheme to work there had been difficult.[4] Elsewhere, the National Farmers' Union expressed concern that dogs were not kept under close control on footpaths as the law requires.[5] This can often result in disturbance to sheep and other stock. It was pointed out that, even if dogs were running around relatively close to their owners, this prevented sheep being grazed for long periods on popular paths. **We believe that dog owners should be encouraged to behave responsibly when on rights of way, through the imposition of fines where necessary.**

---

[1] These principles are adapted from the British Mountaineering policy statement (P Sedgwick January 1990)on repair and maintenance of public paths.
[2] The BUFT was jointly set up by the British Mountaineering Council, Camping and Outdoor Leisure Association (which covers over 400 companies making leisure equipment), the Mountaineering Council of Scotland and the Ramblers' Association.
[3] *Fit for the Future, Report of the National Parks Review Panel*, 1990.
[4] See Annex III.
[5] See Minutes of Evidence of 3 May (National Farmers' Union memorandum).

Guidebooks

122.   At a more local level, it is clear that the publication of certain leaflets and guidebooks featuring recommended walks has increased the use of unsuitable paths,[1] in some cases beyond a sustainable level.[2] While we welcome the publication of information that encourages people to enjoy fresh air and exercise, we believe that the Countryside Commission should encourage discussion between guide book writers, local landowners, National Parks and local authorities to ensure that the routes promoted are sustainable. **We recommend that an award scheme for guidebooks be set up, one of the criteria for an award being the sustainability of the route. Other criteria could be adequate parking near starting points, good access to public transport and the matching of the quality of paths to the likely numbers of users. The Countryside Commission could take responsibility for the administration of such a scheme.**

123.   The Ordnance Survey also has a responsibility to consider these issues in its map publishing policy. In the Peak District National Park, for example, areas which are covered by the Outdoor Leisure maps get far more use than those which are not. We were pleased to hear that there is to be wider map coverage of the Peak District in the near future.[3] **We urge the Ordnance Survey to cover all areas of National Parks and Areas of Outstanding Natural Beauty by Outdoor Leisure maps in the near future.**

Water

124.   Given the limited number of lakes and rivers, and the limited area of coastal waters available for watersports, competition between rival activities is perhaps inevitable. Management and positive planning is therefore particularly necessary. We noted that conflicts between noisy watersports, conservation and 'quiet enjoyment' had been managed effectively in parts of the Cotswold Water Park,[4] where new leisure facilities have been developed in flooded gravel pits.

125.   Our visit to Poole Harbour confirmed that a well-consulted management plan combined with good enforcement can work to everyone's advantage.[5] What has been achieved is commendable, and could be used as an example of good practice (though obviously Poole Harbour is a very large area of water and the Harbour authorities have more resources than other management bodies).

126.   **We note and commend the key features of the management approach to sustainable use of Poole Harbour, embodied in the Aquatic Management Plan, which are:**

—   **An information base covering the different interests, which has recently been extended by survey work on breeding birds and recreational activities;**

—   **A zoning scheme which protects wildlife areas of critical importance but which makes provision for watersports;**

—   **A willingness to amend this scheme in the light of new evidence and in consultation with users;**

—   **The use of bylaws to enforce the zoning scheme; and**

—   **Clear and attractively produced literature which informs users of the regulations and their necessity.**

127.   But there are cases where management will not be enough. As we will state later in this Report, we believe that the planning system should ensure provision for noisy and popular sports in the "Best Available Place."

COUNTRYSIDE MANAGEMENT

EDUCATION

Publicity

128.   We sought to explore with witnesses whether it would be possible to reduce visitor pressure in over-used areas by selectively publicising other, more robust and under-used locations.

129.   The National Farmers' Union suggested that better management of facilities and resources

---

[1] *Ibid.*
[2] Ap 24 para 7(vi).
[3] See Annex II.
[4] See Annex V.
[5] See Annex III.

could be achieved by selectively publicising certain sites in guidebooks and press articles.'[1] Other witnesses pointed to possible problems with this approach. Mr Jo Burgon, Coast and Countryside Adviser, National Trust, stated when giving evidence to the Committee that "[selective marketing] sounds a nice idea but in practice I am not sure whether it actually works...There are so many other influences that are not market-related".[2] Witnesses from the Peak Park Joint Planning Board pointed out that "the problem is other organisations—local authorities, tourist boards, commercial enterprises—who are not under our control; they may continue to advertise the "honey-pots.""[3] The English Tourist Board summarised the situation: "the consumer, at the end of the day, will make his own choice...I do not believe that there is much that one can do to keep people away from certain of those favourite areas."[4]

130.   **We believe that as part of an integrated management strategy, measures should be taken wherever possible to attract visitors to currently under-used robust sites which fit the 'Best Available Place' criteria.**[5] The Department of National Heritage concurred with this view; they suggested that this objective should be achieved in the context of individual operators seeking to develop their own diverse firms, with guidance from government.[6] Considering the problems noted above, we think that if managers are seeking to publicise selected sites as part of an area management plan, they should be able to get specific advice on such publicity and on the suitability of the site from authoritative sources, and we consider that the Department of the Environment and/or the Department of National Heritage should have a duty to provide such information.

Codes of Practice

131.   We note the excellent work done by most governing bodies of sport to produce codes of practice. The evidence shows that the governing body of almost every sport or leisure activity has drawn up a code of practice designed to prevent or minimise damage and nuisance. We also recognise the part local authorities have played. Codes of Practice have also been issued by English Nature (with regard to golf course maintenance) and the Countryside Commission (the Country Code). Most of this advice is clear and sensible, and likely to produce the desired result—if known and followed.

132.   We would like to point out that problems are most likely to arise where people are either unaware of the code or determined to ignore it. It must be remembered that the majority of leisure users of the countryside do not belong to a sporting organisation. The table at the back of this Report shows that whereas an estimated 13 million number of people take rural walks, 100,000 are members of the relevant associations. Various witnesses pointed out that there were many other examples.[7] It is often the mavericks, not affiliated to any recognised body, who cause the problems. In all the areas we visited, some motor and mountain bikes and off-road vehicle users go onto open land and/or use bridleways and green lanes in a manner which startles walkers and horses, churns up the ground and spoils the enjoyment of others.

133.   Nevertheless **codes of practice are useful tools. We therefore believe that it is important to get them disseminated to a much wider audience, providing them to those who are not members of a sporting organisation, via guidebooks, leaflets and manuals. Those who write and sell guidebooks and sporting "how to" books; those who manufacture and sell sports equipment; those who instruct learners or lead parties—all these can, and should, play a part in familiarising their customers with codes of good practice.**

134.   It is clearly an individual decision whether or not to become informed and follow a code of practice. At the same time, encouraging access and leisure use (together with education and information) will get people interested in the natural environment and motivate them to look after it. People who derive benefits from leisure in the countryside must recognise that they also have responsibilities when they are there.

---

[1] See Minutes of Evidence of 3 May (National Farmers Union memorandum)
[2] Q565
[3] Q273
[4] Q841
[5] See para 188.
[6] Q1018.
[7] See Annexes II to VI.

MANAGEMENT AND PARTNERSHIP

135. Whereas the planning system concerns itself with land-use matters, management is concerned with minimising the effects of activity on that land. It is therefore particularly important to have such schemes in place for activities whose effects may vary, such as leisure and tourism.

136. As we have already stated in this Report, we do not believe that at present, leisure activities are the greatest danger to the countryside environment; good management can mitigate their effects. A number of local management schemes were referred to in the written and oral evidence presented to us by local authorities, National Parks and other bodies. In addition, we went on site visits to the Upper Derwent Valley in the Peak District, Derwentwater in the Lake District, the Studland estate of the National Trust and the Cotswold Water Park in order to discuss such schemes in detail.[1]

137. Many of these plans appeared to be the result of careful, and often prolonged, consultation which had successfully identified local problems. All were focused on local solutions, and are to be commended in this respect. Where they were often less successful, however, was in providing built-in mechanisms for evaluating the effectiveness of consultation procedures and for assessing to what extent the plan had been successfully implemented.[2] In this context we were struck by the degree of variation in the acceptance of plans by the local community. It was clear from the evidence we received that the level of co-operation between different organisations responsible for the management of other well-used countryside areas varies considerably. In Purbeck the partnership between local authorities and the National Trust appears to work well. In the New Forest we heard widely differing views from local residents, landowners, the Forestry Commission, the New Forest Committee and local authorities on the extent to which the current arrangements could be relied upon to produce and implement plans for the protection of the New Forest and the New Forest Heritage Area.

138. **We recommend that the Government takes positive steps to encourage the formation of effective partnerships in such areas and that, where the Government is a major landowner, it ensures that Government agencies play a full part in such partnerships.**

139. There are two other issues that we felt should be addressed: the first was the needs of the surrounding area; the second was whether, in managing sensitive and/or popular sites, visitors should be concentrated in one small area, and suitable infrastructure developed there, or encouraged to disperse. This is a decision which needs careful thought based on a shared management philosophy, and a carefully researched consideration of the local area.

140. We commend the work of a rapidly increasing number of local conservation voluntary groups, in particular for the contribution they make to the general public's awareness of the importance of protecting the environment, and also for the practical voluntary work they undertake.

Building Consensus

141. We have previously referred to the successful approach to negotiation initiated by the Lake District National Park Authority in relation to off-road vehicles and mountain bikes. The Environment Council advocates consensus building as "a way of helping people build on common ground, rather than reinforce their differences which often occurs in the traditional problem-solving procedures such as planning inquiries." The Council suggests that this approach increases public understanding and knowledge of the issues, can save time and money and improve the relationship between partners with traditionally conflicting views.[3] **We commend the consensus building approach and consider that consultation in local management schemes should begin at an early stage to overcome some of the cultural conflicts which overshadow any evidence of the environmental impacts of leisure. When such consultation is entered into, efforts must be made to ensure decisions are taken within a reasonable timescale.**

142. **We feel that there are three important criteria upon which to assess the quality of local countryside management schemes:**

   — **They should follow the same general principles as schemes introduced at national and regional level (principles which we suggest elsewhere in this Report);**

---

[1] *Ibid.*
[2] See Annexes II to VI, Q611
[3] Environment Council (Ev not printed).

— **They should clearly have primary regard for the area within the scheme, but not ignore the wider effects they may have; and**

— **After a management scheme is put in place, its effects should be monitored and assessed.**

TRANSPORT MANAGEMENT AND PLANNING

143. We received a substantial amount of evidence related to the planning and management of transport policy at all levels. As with other matters, the benefits of an approach which integrates the provision of public and alternative transport and car parking were stressed. We saw such an approach being taken at a local level in Purbeck and the Lake District.[1] We were pleased to hear that a traffic strategy is being developed by Cumbria County Council, in conjunction with the National Park Authority and the Cumbria Tourist Board, and by Hampshire County Council, New Forest District Council, the New Forest Committee and the Forestry Commission (in the New Forest).[2]

Traffic Restriction Schemes and Park and Ride

144. We accept that there may be a need to restrict cars from certain routes as part of a traffic management strategy. We note that there have been objections to schemes which introduce such restrictions,[3] but would compare such a process to the pedestrianisation of the streets in many cities and towns, which was not done without opposition but has now been found to be successful in some places.

145. We received evidence on the principles behind such proposals from the Countryside Commission[4] and the Association of County Councils,[5] but were disappointed to find very few such schemes actually in operation. There are successful examples in the Goyt Valley, Upper Derwent Valley and the Roaches in the Peak National Park[6] but it must be remembered that these are uniquely topographically suitable areas; their experience cannot be readily translated elsewhere. Attempts to develop demonstration traffic management strategies are also progressing in Cumbria, Surrey, Devon, the Yorkshire Dales and the North York Moors. These include developing a 'road hierarchy' which includes road restrictions.

146. We were disappointed that such schemes are not more widespread. To counter the objections of local businesses when traffic restrictions are proposed, we feel that some sound experimental evidence, as suggested by the Edwards Report,[7] is needed to assess the problems and benefits at a local level where the interests of local tourist businesses (for example bed and breakfasts and teashops) have to be accommodated. We **believe that the Countryside Commission, working in partnership with the Department of Transport, the Rural Development Commission and local groups, should develop its demonstration traffic schemes to comprehensively assess how they tie in with rural transport and the needs of local businesses in a range of tourist locations.**

147. Traffic restriction schemes are often linked to park-and-ride, which involves the provision of buses to take visitors from a car park to, or through, popular beauty spots. Though it does seem an ideal solution to access, the irony is that, though it reduces the squeeze on selected spots, it neither reduces the number of cars in the area nor eliminates the need for car parks; it simply moves the problem around. Another problem is the choice of site for the 'base' car park, which may be controversial.[8] In a few places there is an existing car park that can be used. Elsewhere there is derelict land (old quarries for example) that can be used as a car park, with advantages all round. Here park-and-ride schemes are worthwhile. But in the end, if people are really happy with a bus ride, it makes sense to encourage them to make the whole journey by public transport.[9] **We feel that two or three experimental park-and-ride schemes should be set up on a trial basis, perhaps run in conjunction with the experimental traffic restriction schemes we suggest.**

---

[1] See Annexes III and VI.
[2] See Annexes II and VI.
[3] See Annexes II and VI.
[4] Ev p 158.
[5] Q798.
[6] See Annex II.
[7] *Fit for the Future: Report of the National Parks Review Panel,* Countryside Commission, 1990.
[8] See Annex VI.
[9] See para 153.

Parking

148. In the 1960s and 1970s, parking provision increased to meet demand at certain sites, with car parks designed to hide cars from sight behind trees and bushes: these were supplemented at peak periods by extra parking in fields let out by farmers.[1] We heard evidence that fears about crime have led to car parks now being unscreened so that they are open to view from the road.[2] However, this has opened a new debate about their untidiness and intrusiveness. Casual parking in fields is now discouraged and opposed.[3] In some areas, this has reduced the total amount of parking space available.

149. Rationing car parking may be a method of rationing access to the countryside, and it has also been on occasion a means of visitor charging, with the setting of car park charges higher than running costs.[4] There are inherent dangers and problems with this approach, though we note that the funds raised may help to offset the wider management costs of the site. Limiting parking may simply move the problem on. Failing to get in at one site, the visitors simply move on to another, thus clogging the roads and causing overcrowding somewhere else. People may simply park as near as they can to the car park, either because it is full or because they do not wish to pay the parking charge. This results in the cars stacking up in an unregulated manner, causing congestion and damage to the verges. Such a policy causes ill will. Steps to control car parking away from designated car parks, such as on verges, are to be commended. We also support signposting to encourage vehicles to less traditionally popular areas. However, **as part of a policy to ease pressure on so-called 'honeypot' areas and encourage those less well known it may be appropriate for local consideration to be given to charging above cost for some car parks. Likewise signposting to encourage vehicles away when an area is effectively full should be developed. Additional signposting to encourage visitors to less popular areas should be provided.**

150. **We believe that National Parks, County Councils, authorities covering Areas of Outstanding Natural Beauty, and all other relevant authorities should develop a rural transport strategy. The aims of such a strategy should include:**

— **the provision of new sport and leisure facilities as close to good public transport as possible and near to urban areas;**

— **the development of public transport to eliminate as far as possible the need to use cars for leisure purposes;**

— **the encouragement of cycling;**

— **the recognition that leisure traffic might have to be restricted in some places and under some circumstances;**

— **measures to ensure that lorries and other heavy vehicles are restricted to major routes except for access; and**

— **the opening up to passenger use of existing railway routes.**

151. **Conversely, such strategies should recognise that some people do enjoy looking at scenery from a car window (or, if they are frail or disabled, can only see the countryside this way). The development of good lay-bys and viewpoints would cater for this group. Additionally, some sports and leisure activities necessitate large amounts of equipment and it should be recognised that public transport is unsuitable for groups taking part in these activities.**

152. **We believe that the pressure of visitors, in the end, does need to be catered for, managed and acknowledged. Car parking provision should reflect the level of visitor use which is compatible with environmental protection and the enjoyment of visitors.**

Public and Alternative Transport

153. It is clear that any traffic strategy that involves restrictions necessitates a reconsideration of the role of public transport. Large numbers of people used trains and buses for leisure purposes before the Second World War. We would suggest that measures be made to help them to do so again; by making the journey more 'fun' and certainly by making it more reliable and convenient.

---

[1] See Annex VI.
[2] See Annex III.
[3] See Annex II.
[4] Ev p 200.

154.   When giving evidence, a witness from the Department of Transport stated that the provision of practical applications for transport in the countryside was "quite difficult."[1] They pointed firstly to the powers of local authorities to supplement public transport and secondly to the Rural Development Fund administered by the Rural Development Commission, which may finance such schemes.[2] **We feel further efforts should come from Government to develop and encourage local authorities to develop rural transport for leisure purposes within available resources.**

155.   We also feel that local authorities should play their part. We commend the Peak Park for their efforts in encouraging visitors from Manchester and Sheffield to use the train to Edale, and then take a linking bus service, and the efforts made by the Purbeck Heritage Committee to re-open closed sections of railway line between Wareham and Swanage. We do, however, regret that even with such efforts there are not now considerably more off-peak trains to Edale than there were in the 1930s.[3]

156.   The popular ferry service on Derwentwater is an example of making public transport part of the visit experience. It was stressed to us that many walkers use the ferry at the start and end of their day.[4]

157.   The encouragement of cycling is also important. Leisure cycling can reduce car traffic and encourage people to explore the countryside in a peaceful and healthy way.[5] The development of cycle hire facilities is welcome, and we commend the schemes that we saw in the Peak National Park.[6] We would like to see more of these. For those who wish to take their cycles with them, **we urge rail operators to maintain and improve facilities for carrying cycles on trains, especially in National Parks.**[7]

158.   It is also necessary to provide safe and pleasant routes along which people can cycle. We note the efforts made in the Peak Park to use the routes of old railway lines—the 'Monsal Trail' and the 'Tissington Trail'—as routes for cycles, horses and walkers.[8] We also welcome the efforts of Sustrans to promote a network of national safe cycleways.

Off-Road Vehicles

159.   We hope that local negotiations between the Land Access and Recreation Association, local highway authorities and management bodies will be successful in finding ways of permitting four-wheel drive vehicles to use most green lanes without causing the lanes to deteriorate further, spoiling them for other users or making life intolerable for local residents and without resorting to expensive Traffic Regulation Orders which are hard to enforce. If this approach is to succeed (and especially if there is an increase in the number of drivers interested in rough terrain driving), land must be made available for this activity.

160.   A cause for concern is that although the Land Access and Recreation Association have a Code of Practice, it is not always observed. We regret that some companies, for example Land Rover,[9] do not draw buyers' attention to this Code of Practice. We would also note that some businesses selling four-wheel drive vehicles are training drivers on routes which cannot sustain such use.[10] We approve of training facilities being set up, but we regret that some are not fully environmentally conscious. **We recommend that retailers of four-wheel drive vehicles, whether new or second-hand, draw purchasers' attention to the Land Access and Recreation Association and its code of conduct for off-road vehicles, and we commend those who already do so. We also recommend that organisations involved in training four-wheel drive users produce a Code of Practice in consultation with the Land Access and Recreation Association.**

161.   With regard to local authorities and the re-designation of certain routes, **we recommend that National Park and Highway authorities initiate collaborative negotiations between motoring organisations, other rights of way users and local communities in seeking management solutions to the use of green lanes before resorting to statutory traffic controls.**

---

[1]   Q58.

[2]   Q59.

[3]   There were 32 weekend trains between Sheffield and Manchester (8am to 8pm) in the summer of 1938; there are 37 this summer (1995).

[4]   See Annex VI.

[5]   Ap 23.

[6]   See Annex II.

[7]   Ap 11.

[8]   See Annex II.

[9]   Q741.

[10]   See Annex VI.

Other Motorsports

162. In the past, rallying has caused some controversy, and we received some evidence about it (see impacts table). Much of the evidence we received, however, pointed to the measures put in place by the Land Access and Recreation Association, the Forestry Commission, the Ramblers' Association, and other interested bodies which will enable large numbers of people to enjoy the sport without either damaging the natural environment or causing unreasonable problems for other people.[1] Similarly the governing bodies of motorbike scrambling and trail riding seem keen to make their activities acceptable. We have already noted the problems these groups outlined about 'maverick' individuals giving the sport a bad name.[2]

163. Meanwhile **we believe that codes of practice and a framework of voluntary co-operation are part of the way forward for the management of motorsports in rural areas and we commend all who have established such initiatives. We have to stress, however, that there will be some conflicts until firstly, quieter machines are developed and used and, secondly, a balance is struck between allowing vehicles on legal routes, providing suitable land for informal motorsports, and preventing the illegal use of land elsewhere.**

MISCELLANEOUS LEISURE ISSUES

General Development Order: the 28 and 14 Day rule

164. The Town and Country Planning General Development Order 1988 gives a general 'grant' of planning permission for certain activities which "are judged to be sufficiently minor or temporary [such] that specific planning permission is unnecessary."[3] This includes the use of land for leisure activities for up to 28 days in any calendar year, apart from the holding of markets and motor car and motorcycle racing, for which use is limited to 14 days. The Order excludes the temporary use of land within Sites of Special Scientific Interest for motor car and motorcycle racing "including trials of speed, and practising," war games, or clay pigeon shooting.[4] We received a substantial amount of evidence on the operation of these rights.

165. A local planning authority may make an 'Article 4 Direction'[5] to withdraw these rights. These directions require the Secretary of State's approval if they are to remain in force for more than six months. Department of the Environment Circular 9/95 states that "permitted development rights have been endorsed by Parliament and consequently should not be withdrawn locally without compelling reasons."[6] If such a Direction is made, those with an interest in the land can apply for planning permission in the normal way. If permission is refused the planning authority may be liable to pay compensation to them "for abortive expenditure, or other loss and damage directly attributable to the withdrawal of permitted development rights."[7] For example, we were told by the Peak Park Joint Planning Board that they had made an £8,000 one-off payment after an Article 4 Direction had been made to restrict cycle scrambling.[8]

Rights for Noisy Activities

166. Several witnesses expressed their concerns about the operation of such rights for 'noisy' activities, for example clay-pigeon shooting and motor-cycle trials. Mr Terry Robinson, Head of Recreation and Access at the Countryside Commission, stated that the number of days' use permitted under it should be reduced;[9] the Chief Executive of English Nature, Dr Langslow, stated that these activities should be brought within the planning system.[10] The National Trust proposed that the General Development Order 1988 be strengthened and certain activities, such as clay pigeon shooting, temporary use of land for caravan sites and war games removed from the category of permitted

---

[1] Ev p 171.
[2] See para 132.
[3] Ev p 35.
[4] S.I.,1995 No. 418 Part 4 Class B.1.
[5] So-called because the power it refers to is outlined in Article 4 of the Order.
[6] Circular 9/95, Appendix D, para 1.
[7] Circular 9/95, Appendix D, para 2.
[8] QQ279-282.
[9] Q431.
[10] Q423.

development within National Parks and Areas of Outstanding Natural Beauty (AONBs) as well as Sites of Special Scientific Interest.[1]

167.   With regard to clay pigeon shooting, the Department of the Environment stated that after consultation in 1993 they had decided that temporary rights for clay pigeon shooting should remain, and had encouraged the relevant bodies to agree a Code of Practice to limit noise nuisance.[2] They did not mention any plans to address the issue of whether such rights should be withdrawn in National Parks and Areas of Outstanding Natural Beauty.

168.   **We feel that there is a need to address the issue of permitted rights again, both in terms of noise nuisance and possible environmental damage. We support efforts to introduce a voluntary code of practice with regard to clay pigeon shooting and suggest that it is completed and introduced as soon as practicable. We would suggest that a suitable time to re-examine the system would be after such a Code of Practice has been in place for 12 months and that it be made clear that if many unfavourable submissions are received these rights will be withdrawn.**

169.   We also received evidence concerning the pattern of operation of these rights. These included complaints that due to different rights being used on different fields, nearby houses were subject to noise nuisance for much more than 28 days of the year.[3] We believe that this issue needs to be resolved. The review we suggest above should include an examination of how it could be addressed.

Contributions

170.   **We commend initiatives to remedy damage caused by leisure activities through voluntary contributions, especially those which relate to a specific project. For example, we thought that the 'Our Man at the Top' scheme in the Lake District, which collects donations to pay the wages of a footpath restoration worker was particularly worthwhile. We also commend the measures to educate and inform those who donated to this scheme.**

171.   **Schemes which encourage and enable contributions to be made by industry are also a welcome development.** The British Upland Footpath Trust, which is mentioned elsewhere in this Report, is a scheme of this type.[4] **We see a case for voluntary contributions in assisting in the cost of providing visitor facilities and maintenance of scenically important areas.**

Individual Responsibility

172.   As we stated earlier in this Report, it is often the few maverick individuals involved in an activity who cause most of the problems. However, we can all be careless when in the countryside; it is easy to forget our sense of responsibility when we are on our 'day off.' Things could be a great deal better if we all played our part and acknowledged that we can make a difference in the impacts we make and act accordingly. **Leisure time is something people treasure; and spending it in the countryside creates a sense of freedom that relieves weekday stresses. However, we should not forget that how and where we spend our leisure not only affects other people, but may have consequences for the future of the natural environment.**

ENVIRONMENTAL ISSUES AND PRINCIPLES

SUSTAINABLE DEVELOPMENT

173.   Since the "Earth Summit" at Rio de Janeiro in 1992 the political consensus has been in favour of sustainable development. One example of this is that, many witnesses emphasised that recreational, sporting and leisure activities/developments in the countryside had to be "sustainable."[5] The clearest definition of sustainable development is set out in the Brundtland report:[6] "Sustainable development is development that meets the needs of the present without compromising the ability of future generations to meet their needs." We strongly agree with this principle. But how should it be

---

[1] Ev p 201.
[2] See Minutes of Evidence of 10 May (Department of the Environment supplementary evidence, para 16).
[3] Ap 48.
[4] see para 118.
[5] QQ365, 585, 716, 782, 817, 937-938, Ev pp 109,137, British Trust for Conservation Volunteers, Leisure and Rural Development Research Group, Sheffield Centre for Ecology and Environmental Management,Tourism Concern (Ev not printed).
[6] Ap 48.

interpreted when it comes to the interaction of tourism and the environment? Witnesses were largely unable to show us practical applications of the principle or to suggest in detail how it might be interpreted in terms of policy.

174.   An early formulation of the principle in this context may be found in the Sandford Report: here it states that public enjoyment of National Parks must be such "as will leave their natural beauty unimpaired for the enjoyment of future generations."[1] The Council for the Protection of Rural England would seem to interpret this in almost absolutist terms: "the environment has an intrinsic value which outweighs its value as a tourist asset and ... tourism must not be allowed to damage this resource.[2] In oral evidence to us, however, the Secretary of State for National Heritage, defining his Department as "The sponsoring department for an industry that is the fourth largest wealth-creating sector in Britain"[3] gave an interpretation with an economic twist—it would be (economically) counterproductive to allow tourist development and activity to spoil the landscape people came to enjoy.[4] Similarly, the Minister of State for the Environment and Countryside stressed that any environmental damage done by tourism was "killing the goose that laid the golden egg."[5]

175.   English Nature's position appears to fall between these two extremes, but they argue that "In relation to leisure activities the achievement of environmental sustainability means integrating environmental consequences into all levels of policy formulation, development and land-use planning."[6] More cautiously formulated, Department of the Environment Planning Policy Guidance states that "The sum total of decisions in the planning field...should not deny future generations the best of today's environment."[7] The Royal Town Planning Institute, however, drew attention to what they see as a difference between conservation and sustainability. Conservation is what has been happening to date, though ironically their definition of conservation is very similar to that of other organisations' definition of sustainability: "The wise use and continuance of supply of a scarce resource." However, the principle of sustainability, they argue, moves the argument forward from this, so that the desideratum is not merely trying to strike a balance between conservation and development but "catering for the needs of the present without compromising the environment for future generations."[8] The inclusion of the term 'catering for' gives a novel twist to discussions of sustainability. Whereas from Sandford onwards the principal concern has been for future generations, this new interpretation calls for consideration of the claims of present generations too. It is in agreement with Brundtland which refers to "the needs of the present" as well as "the ability of future generations to meet their needs." Broadly speaking, we support this interpretation.

176.   On the one hand, we would suggest that the principle of sustainability should entail the protection of the environment from inappropriate use and/or excessive recreational use which might compromise it in the future. But, on the other hand, it should not be forgotten that leisure and tourist activities also need to be catered for in the present. Though the environment should not be compromised by thoughtless recreational development, legitimate leisure should not be squeezed out of the countryside and National Parks. Our proposed interpretation of sustainability cuts both ways.

177.   This is especially the case when calls for the restriction of recreational activities are based on unfounded ideas of environmental damage or the desire for a tidy or picturesque landscape. It must be remembered that much of Britain's heritage was not sustainable in its originally designed form, anyway. Traditional stone walls in upland farming areas were never sustainable as field boundaries; stone castles, after a very short military life, crumbled to picturesque ruins. These and countless others have lived a much longer life as landscape features and tourist attractions than as functional artefacts. Tracks over peat, field paths, riverside walks, all of their nature come and go, shift and change. Hill farms pushed out their boundaries in response to wartime shortages well beyond what was sustainable in terms of labour, man hours and terrain. The landscape is not unchangeable and the ideal of sustainability should not lead to conserving it in an artificial time-capsule.

178. It is necessary, then, to separate the real from the imaginary problemsand to step back from seeing change as necessarily a threat. Within this outlook,the sustainability principle could mean, not

---

[1] *Report of the Sandford Committee,* 1974.
[2] Ev p 137.
[3] Q939.
[4] *Ibid.*
[5] Q952.
[6] Ev p 109.
[7] PPG 1 para 3.
[8] *Extracts from Rural Planning in the 1990s: A rural planning policy framework prepared by the Countryside Panel.* Royal Town Planning Institute memorandum, Appendix 1.

the fossilisation of the countryside, but a way of meeting leisure needs which not only does not cause problems but positively enhances the environment where it can and uses leisure activities as a way of increasing people's understanding and appreciation of the world around them.

179. **We would like to draw attention to the interpretation of the sustainability principle put forward by the Royal Town Planning Institute in their document "Rural Planning in the 1990s[1] and which refers to the need to:**

— **adopt the precautionary approach to planning matters likely to have environmental impact;**

— **consider the ability of the countryside to absorb development without detriment to the social and physical environment;**

— **preserve the integrity of environmental systems across the full range of their natural distribution;**

— **promote a self-sustaining rural economy;**

— **maintain the character of rural communities; and**

— **ensure that the countryside has its own dynamic and integrity, and is not "simply a contrived facade for the amusement of visitors.[2]**

GREEN TOURISM

180. The concept of "green tourism" is closely allied with that of sustainability. Indeed, the two terms are often used interchangeably (and sometimes a little vaguely). We believe that green tourism should be defined and supported by a practical code (arising from the principle of sustainable development), to which planning matters can be referred.

181. Witnesses stated in their evidence to us that the concept of green tourism "is now widespread."[3] We note that the English Tourist Board have been producing a number of practical guides to operators to promote good practice, including "Green Light: a Guide to Sustainable Tourism", "Tourism in National Parks," and a guide for caravan and holiday park operators.[4] We also note the English Tourist Board's present project to produce a "definitive guide to sustainable development"[5] based on a number of pilot projects. Nineteen projects have been sponsored at a cost of £935,000[6] and their effectiveness is presently being assessed.[7] We hope that this assessment does not merely summarise the projects, but draws together common themes which could be applied in a variety of situations.

182. Some groups have expressed fears that the concept of green tourism may be used to enforce arbitrary, and sometimes uneconomic ideas of what constitutes "acceptable" uses of rural land. The National Farmers' Union, for example, believes "that concepts such as green tourism represent too narrow a basis for future development and an overly protective approach to countryside recreational use."[8] As we have already said, whilst we believe that the environment should be protected from excessive and thoughtless leisure development, we also believe that leisure should not be squeezed out of the countryside in response to environmental panic.

183. In general, we would suggest that "green tourism" might at best mean using tourism to promote and enhance the environment; at worst, it would at least involve striking a balance between conflicting interests.

184. **The Government adopted the following environmental objectives in the light of the 'Tourism Task Force' Report:[9]**

— **to support the development of leisure in ways which contribute to, rather than detract from the quality of our environment;**

---

[1] *Ibid.*
[2] *Extracts from Rural Planning in the 1990s: A rural planning policy framework prepared by the Countryside Panel.* Royal Town Planning Institute memorandum, Appendix 1.
[3] Ap 24 para 11.
[4] Q938.
[5] Ev p22.
[6] Q954.
[7] Q938.
[8] See Minutes of Evidence of 3 May (National Farmers Union memorandum)
[9] See para 76.

— to promote environmental quality issues within the leisure industries as well as issues concerned with the quality of their services and products;

— to ensure that all leisure managers become increasingly aware of visitor management techniques and ways of protecting the environment whilst protecting their industry; and

— to encourage and disseminate those forms of tourism, sport and recreation which in themselves aim to safeguard the environment."[1]

We commend these objectives.

185.   With these in mind, the following table draws together some of the written evidence to form practical applications of "green tourism":

Accommodating "leisure uses ... which cause no significant damage to the resources they use and preferably contribute to their conservation".[2]

Using the intrinsic nature of an area rather than importing "attractions".[3]

Encouraging "low impact" tourism requiring minimum development and promoting the understanding of the countryside.[4]

Developing planning procedures aimed at conserving "environmental resources" rather than consuming them.[5]

Assessing the environmental impacts of proposed developments.[6]

Guiding new developments away from sensitive sites to locations where fewer environmental impacts may occur.[7]

Encouraging designs for tourist developments which are themselves good examples of environmental principles (with, for example, access by public transport, efficient use of energy, water and habitat), drawing attention to these features on site by relevant means.[8]

Persuading tourist operators that "green" is not only best for the environment but a positive selling point.[9]

Reusing traditional buildings for tourist accommodation.[10]

Developing riding, walking and cycling along vehicle-free routes.[11]

Developing education opportunities.[12]

Creating public awareness of the problems that can arise out of tourism and leisure.[13]

Using tourism/tourist sites/information centres etc to publicise general codes of conduct such as the country code or relevant specialist codes of practice.[14]

Siting new developments in towns or on the urban fringe, thereby using tourism to assist efforts to control rural traffic.[15]

Using tourism to open up/restore alternative modes of transport (canals, horsedrawn vehicles, railways, etc.[16]

---

[1] Ev p 4.
[2] Ev p 79.
[3] Ap 24 para 11.
[4] Ap 45.
[5] *Extracts from Rural Planning in the 1990s: A rural planning policy framework prepared by the Countryside Panel.* Royal Town Planning Institute memorandum, Appendix 1.
[6] Ap 45.
[7] *Ibid.*
[8] Ap 44.
[9] *Ibid.*
[10] *Ibid.*
[11] *Ibid.*
[12] *Ibid.*
[13] Ap 24 para 12.
[14] See Minutes of Evidence of 3 May (Royal Town Planning Institute memorandum).
[15] See para 187.
[16] See para 143.

186. We think that conditions of sustainable tourism may be met by applying concepts of "green tourism" at both national and local levels, by the promotion of positive planning within the planning system and by emphasising the role of management, partnership and education.

"BEST AVAILABLE PLACE" PRINCIPLE

187. We would suggest a 'Best Available Place' criterion for new leisure facilities.

188. As we stated elsewhere in this Report, leisure developments can improve landscapes and local habitats.[1] **The 'Best Available Place' would be where new facilities:**
   — **are needed;**
   — **are as near to where the main users live as possible;**
   — **use derelict land, or where this is not available, land of the least agricultural, ecological and scenic value; and**
   — **are developed with regard to the environmental suitability of the site, conducting an environmental assessment or consulting with English Nature where appropriate.**

189. **It should also be remembered that many towns and cities have good family facilities in their urban parks. It is important that these are well maintained and policed to keep them safe and pleasant. As the Institute of Leisure Amenity Management recommended, "urban greenspace and open spaces [should be improved] in order that they can provide the experience of the countryside in the town."[2]**

CONCLUSION

190. In summary, we would note that:
   — evidence for growth in leisure pressure in recent years is limited although there have been changes in the pattern;
   — evidence on the impact of leisure on the environment suggests that it is not as bad as is often made out and that much of the conflict arises from cultural perceptions;
   — the planning system does have an important role in minimising any adverse impacts but in itself is not enough to counter all the pressures that arise, and should provide a more positive guide in providing for difficult activities;
   — management activity is necessary to supplement the planning process if the environment is to be conserved and leisure users enabled to benefit from the countryside. There is a need to continue to encourage good management practice and develop new approaches in the case of major issues such as traffic and water management;
   — the ability of people to enjoy all forms of leisure appropriate to the countryside should not be constrained unless there are pressing reasons for restricting that activity. Where restrictions are necessary, there is an onus to provide alternative facilities to meet demand; and
   — any new provision in the countryside should have regard to sustainable principles which includes the recognition of the need to make provision for both current and future generations.

---

[1] See para 31.
[2] Ap 30.

ADMINISTRATION, LEGISLATION AND DESIGNATIONS

The two Government departments with the greatest interest in this area are the Department of the Environment and the Department of National Heritage. The DNH is the sponsoring Department for tourism, and the DoE's role, as it is in relation to any industry, is to protect the environment from any harmful effects of the industry.

The Department of Transport deals with local transport and road policy;[1] the Department of Health aims to promote physical activity and countryside recreation as part of its 'Health of the Nation' programme[2] and the Ministry of Agriculture, Fisheries and Food has wide ranging relevant responsibilities, including the promotion of an effective agricultural industry, the protection and enhancement of the rural environment, the economic and social interests of rural areas and the promotion of the enjoyment of the countryside by the public.[3] The Forestry Commission[4] is responsible for advising on and implementing forestry policy.

The Maastricht Treaty in 1992 first acknowledged that European Community action should include measures in this area; recent developments have included the publication of a Green Paper on the role of the Union in the field of tourism.[5]

STATUTORY BODIES

As the Department of the Environment's memorandum states, much of the policy formulated by Departments is implemented by various statutory agencies.[6]

SPONSORED BY THE DEPARTMENT OF THE ENVIRONMENT

The British Waterways Board is responsible for the maintenance and operation of over 2,000 miles of river and canals in England, Wales and Scotland. It is the country's largest navigation authority.[7]

The Countryside Commission describe their role as "the Government's principal adviser on the conservation of the English countryside and its enjoyment by people."[8] They own no land or facilities but aim to work with others to achieve three broad aims:

> "To conserve and enhance the scenic, natural, historic and cultural qualities of the whole countryside; to secure and extend opportunities for people to enjoy and use the countryside for open-air recreation; and to promote understanding of the countryside, its life and work, and in carrying [these duties] out [the Countryside Commission] has regard to the needs of agriculture and forestry and the economic and social needs of the countryside."[9]

The Countryside Commission is also responsible for the designation of Areas of Outstanding Natural Beauty.

English Nature is "responsible for advising both central and local government on nature conservation and for promoting the wildlife and natural features of England."[10] This includes the establishment, maintenance and management of National Nature Reserves and the identification, notification and promotion of the conservation of Sites of Special Scientific Interest (SSSIs).[11]

English Nature is also responsible for commissioning a substantial amount of research projects "relevant to nature conservation",[12] some of which relate to the impacts of leisure activities on the countryside environment and can be found elsewhere in this Report.[13]

---

[1] Ev p 4
[2] Ev p 5
[3] All of these had input into the memorandum by the DoE
[4] Ap Ev p 171
[5] COM(95) 97
[6] Ev p 2
[7] Ev p 4
[8] Ev p 150
[9] Ev p 150
[10] Ev p 105
[11] Ev p 105
[12] Ev p 1
[13] See Impacts Table

The National Rivers Authority[1] has statutory duties and powers under the 1991 Water Resources Act which include recreation, conservation and navigation throughout England and Wales. The Authority outline their specific duties for conservation as including "to further and enhance flora and fauna (etc.) of special interest", which they say "implies a positive obligation towards conservation".[2] The NRA also has a general duty to promote amenity and recreation on the land and water in its control, and issues more than 1 million rod licences to anglers across England and Wales each year,[3] and 40,000 boat licences.

The Rural Development Commission[4] "advise the Government on the economic and social development of England's rural areas." The Department of the Environment notes that "in some rural communities tourism and leisure activities may make the difference between closure and viability for shops, pubs and other vital services."[5]

BODIES SPONSORED BY THE DEPARTMENT OF NATIONAL HERITAGE

The British Tourist Authority's aims are "to maximise tourism receipts from overseas visitors" and it also "advises Government and public bodies on matters affecting inward tourism in Britain."

The English Tourist Board's remit is "to maximise receipts from domestic tourism and underpin the British Tourist Authority's marketing overseas by providing leadership to the industry." The English Tourist Board passes on 'about half' of its grant-in-aid to the twelve non-statutory Regional Tourist Boards in England.[6]

Departmental expenditure on the English Tourist Board was £16.2 million in 1992–93; it is expected to fall to £11.3 million in 1994–95 and £10.0 million each in 1995–96 and 1996–97. The Department of National Heritage pointed out in their 1994 Annual Report that the non-Government funding to the English Tourist Board in 1992–93 had increased 15 per cent on the previous year.[7]

The Sports Council has, as part of its remit, a "responsibility for promoting and fostering sport and active recreation in the countryside."[8] Through its 'Sport for All' campaigns it has had a role in formal and informal outdoor pursuits. It has also been involved in the preparation of regional and tourism sports strategies, through its own regional offices and the work of the Regional Councils for Sport and Recreation, to which those offices provide the secretariat.

Under restructuring proposals announced in July 1994 two new bodies will be set up, the English Sports Council and the United Kingdom Sports Council. At the same time, the focus for the Sports Council's direct grant will be concentrated on "young people, the pursuit of excellence and the effective distribution of National Lottery funds".[9]

REGIONAL BODIES

The Regional Councils for Sport and Recreation were set up in 1976 as successor bodies to the Regional Sports Councils and consist of representatives from the public and voluntary sectors. There are 10 such "RCSRs" in England.[10] They are responsible for preparing regional strategies for sport and recreation.

It has been announced that the Government intends to cease the formal linkages between the Regional Councils for Sport and Recreation and the regional Sports Council offices on 1 January 1996.

The Regional Tourist Boards, of which there are twelve in England, are non-statutory public bodies. They work with the English Tourist Board in the dissemination of good practice and guidance to the

---

[1] Ap 38
[2] *Ibid*
[3] *Ibid*
[4] Ap 47
[5] Ev p 3
[6] Chapter 9, Department of National Heritage Annual Report 1994 (Cm 2511)
[7] Chapter 9 para 912, *op cit*
[8] Ev p 23
[9] Ev p 22
[10] Northern Region, Yorkshire and Humberside Region, North West Region, West Midlands Region, East Midland Region, Eastern Region, Greater London Region, South East Region, Southern Region, South Western Region

industry; promote and advertise the attractions of their area and also prepare Regional Tourism Strategies.

National Park Authorities' primary function is to further Park purposes whilst having regard to the social and economic well-being of the area. Two thirds of the members of National Park Boards and committees are appointed by the county councils and district councils in whose areas the National Parks lie; the remaining third by the Secretary of State. Two National Parks, the Peak District and the Lake District, are run by independent Planning Boards, the others are run by committees of the constituent county and district councils.

NPAs work in the fields of conservation, planning recreation and the provision of information. They are also responsible for the preparation of local, waste and minerals plans for the whole of their area, and the receipt, registration and determination of planning applications, including those for minerals and waste.[1] Other responsibilities include land management, information and interpretation services and administration.

Local Authorities are responsible for the implementation of the planning system, provide public facilities for recreation and leisure, and many also have local highway and public rights of way responsibilities.[2] These include the power to make orders extinguishing the right to use vehicles on a highway[3] and to make Traffic Regulation Orders,[4] the making of the latter is somewhat restricted by the cost—about £4,000 per Order.[5] Local authorities are also involved in the provision of public transport as they consider appropriate and which would not otherwise be provided.[6] They are also responsible for the control of outdoor advertisements.[7]

The Local Government Act 1972 gave local authorities powers to work with the English Tourist Board and other statutory bodies in order to develop tourism in their areas.[8] Some authorities have produced plans and strategies for tourism.[9] They also have powers under the Countryside Act 1968 to create country parks and control and regulate activities within them.

DESIGNATED AREAS

Areas of Outstanding Natural Beauty: There are 40 Areas of Outstanding Natural Beauty (AONBs) in England and Wales, so designated to protect their landscape importance. They cover a larger area in England than the National Parks—20,198 sq km as opposed to 9,631 sq km. AONBs are designated by the Countryside Commission, subject to confirmation by the Secretary of State under Section 87 of the National Parks and Access to the Countryside Act 1949. The most recent AONB to be designated was Nidderdale in North Yorkshire on 14 February 1994. This, according to the Department of the Environment is "one of the last AONBs in the [Countryside] Commission's designation programme."

Heritage Coasts: There are also 45 Heritage Coasts in England and Wales, covering 1,525 km or 35 per cent of the coastline.[10]

Other designations: Other sites have been designated for protection of rare species and diversity of flora and fauna. These include Sites of Special Scientific Interest (SSSIs) which accounted for 19,431 sq km at the end of 1994.[11] SSSIs can either be notified under the Wildlife and Countryside Act 1981 or by management agreements between site owners and English Nature. National Nature Reserves, also established under legislation accounted for 1,895 sq km. Other sites are protected under international obligations, such as Special Protection Areas for birds (SPAs) and Wetlands of International Importance under the Ramsar Convention (3,126 and 3,456 sq km at the end of 1994 respectively).

---

[1] P 20, Local Government Review : The Functions of Local Government in England
[2] Ev p 18, 252
[3] Under the Town and Country Planning Act 1990
[4] These procedures are laid down by the Local Authorities' Traffic Orders (Procedure) (England and Wales) Regulations 1989 and The Road Traffic (Temporary Restrictions)
[5] Q 996
[6] Under the Transport Acts 1968 and 1985
[7] Under the Provisions of the Town and Country Planning (Control of Advertisements) Regulations 1992, which are made under the Town and Country Planning Act 1990
[8] *Local Government Review : The Functions of Local Authorities In England, DoE*
[9] For example the New Forest District Council's "Living with the Enemy" project
[10] DoE, Digest of Environmental Statistics No. 17 1995
[11] *Ibid*

RELEVANT LEGISLATION

National Parks and Access to the Countryside Act 1949: Made provision for National Parks and created a National Parks Commission; conferred powers on the Nature Conservancy and local authorities to establish and maintain nature reserves; made further provision for recording, creation, maintenance and improvement of public paths and securing access to open country.

Countryside Act 1968: Enlarged the functions of the National Parks Commission and renamed it the Countryside Commission; conferred new powers on local authorities and other bodies for the conservation and enhancement of natural beauty; and amended the classification process of footpaths, bridleways and other public paths.

Wildlife and Countryside Act 1981: Amended the law relating to the Countryside Commission; provided for the setting up of Sites of Special Scientific Interest, National and Marine Nature Reserves and abandoned the 'suitability test' for reclassification of Rights of Way.

ANNEX II

Note by the Specialist Adviser

VISIT TO THE PEAK DISTRICT NATIONAL PARK ON 8-9 MARCH 1995

BACKGROUND

Members of the Environment Committee visited the Peak District as part of their inquiry into the Environmental Impact of Leisure Activities. The party consisted of:

Mr Andrew Bennett (Chairman)
Mr Robert Ainsworth
Mr Geoffrey Clifton-Brown
Mr John Denham
Mr Harold Elletson
Helen Jackson
Mr Michael Stephen
Mr Roy Thomason

Ms Sarah Adams (Assistant Clerk)
Ms Melanie Sault (Secretary)
Mr Geoff Broom (Specialist Adviser)
Mr Roger Sidaway (Specialist Adviser)

WEDNESDAY 8 MARCH

The Committee travelled to Macclesfield where it was met by *Chris Harrison,* the National Park Officer, *Patricia Goodall McIntosh*, Director of Visitor Services, *Geoff Howe,* the area ranger and other members of the ranger service.

The Roaches

The party then proceeded to the Roaches on the western side of the Park. The area is popular with walkers and climbers, the gritstone cliffs having an international reputation for climbing. Some concerns were expressed by the Park Authority about substantial increases in the volume of climbers, and in particular the use of the site for televised climbs. The area was acquired by the National Park in 1980 when it was suffering from overstocking and increasing leisure use, following failure to agree a management agreement with the farmer/owners who had purchased the land on the demise of the previous estate owner in 1976.

Problems with parking and congestion increased in the 1980s. The National Park Authority created a lay-by alongside the main access to the climbing area. However, parking along the road caused considerable difficulties for through traffic, occasionally blocking the road to emergency vehicles. The National Park therefore undertook an initiative in 1994 whereby parking restrictions were introduced along a section of the road close to the climbing area, and a park and ride service was introduced at weekends during the summer season.

The park and ride operates from a Severn Trent Water car park at Titterworth Reservoir. The service operates every 30 minutes on Sundays and Bank Holidays from Easter to October, and on Saturdays between May and September, with approximately 11 return journeys on Saturdays and double the number on Sundays. In the main season, average daily passenger numbers on Saturdays varied from 60 to 106, dropping to between 30 and 63 in the off peak season. Comparable carryings on Sundays were up to 336 at the peak season and between 60 and 170 in the off peak period. The service is provided free by the National Park at an annual cost of £14,300. Severn Trent do however charge a car parking fee of 50p. The cost of running the bus service was £3,300 for the Saturday service and £11,000 for the Sunday service, and the initiative is receiving support from the Countryside Commission.

The police enforce no parking restrictions and have responded to any problems. There has been little change in traffic flows between Monday and Saturday, but average flows on Sundays are down by 100 vehicles. The scheme has little impact on the attractiveness of the area, and the road has remained open. However, the impact of the parking restrictions has been to displace parking further down the road, so consideration is being given to extending them. The level of climbing activity has remained the same with climbers either arriving early and parking in the lay-by or walking in to the site. However there is a potential problem of theft occurring in the car park, which is of concern to some climbers.

The Park Authority had also separately purchased Rockall Cottage on the site which had become semi-derelict. The Cottage has been converted into a bothy for up to 12 people and is booked for every weekend over the next two years. The British Mountaineering Council had contributed to the costs as a memorial to Don Whillans.

Goyt Valley

The party then proceeded, passing the Goyt Valley, the location of an earlier traffic management experiment dating back to 1976. The original scheme involved closure of the road up the valley, and the provision of a bus service from the car park at the entry to the valley. However, use of the bus service had declined and it had therefore been withdrawn. The road was still shut on Sundays and bank holidays in the summer, with one way traffic at other times. There were no residents or commercial businesses directly affected by the initiative.

At lunch a number of issues were discussed informally including the possibility of closing roads where visitor pressures were acute. Although such initiatives had been taken by the Park Authority at the Goyt Valley and in the Upper Derwent Valley, neither area contained commercial enterprises.

A current case being considered by the Park Authority involved a road with a shop. The County Council, as highway authority, was in favour of closing the road but such a move would substantially affect the shop's trade. The Park Authority were wary of subsidising the shop to compensate for the loss of trade because of the precedent this would create. The Park Authority owns a pub elsewhere which is let at reduced rent, reflecting conditions attached to the operation of the establishment.

Dovedale

Following lunch, the party visited Dovedale accompanied by Ken Parker, Director of Management Services. Dovedale is one of the most popular sites in the Park, being visited by around 2 million visitors a year. The pressure of visitors had caused increasing problems of congestion as a result of roadside parking, while car parking was also spreading onto hillside land intruding on the character of the site. Walkers and cars had intermingled on the road leading up to the stepping stones at the road further up the valley. The National Park Authority in consultation with the major landowners had therefore developed a visitor management scheme. The main elements included:

— Rationalisation and reduction in the car parking provision in the area. Roadside car parking and permission for parking on the hillside were removed and the remaining car park at the entrance to the Dale was rationalised.

— Car park areas were extended at Thorpe and on the Tissington Trail, and a new car park provided at Blore.

— A coach lay-by was provided at the entrance to the valley.

— The toilet block at the main car park was acquired by the National Park Authority and extended and improved; and

— The footpath was segregated from the road carriageway in the lower part of the valley.

The capital costs of undertaking the scheme were largely borne by the National Park Authority. The car park remains in private hands with income from car parking being taken by the owner.

A footbridge across the river close to the car park provides access to the footpath on the west bank of the river away from the carriageway. However, many people used the footbridge to gain direct access to Thorpe Cloud, resulting in substantial erosion and intrusive scarring on the hillside. The National Trust has diverted that route by the use of fencing across the line of the scarring and the hillside has now largely recovered, although the fencing remains in place. The car park at Blore is relatively small and provides for local use as well as visitors. In order to ensure that it is not used for long stay visits, there is a 45 minute parking restriction which is difficult to enforce effectively.

The National Park Authority has now put forward further proposals to close the road entirely north of the car park entrance and to relocate the footbridge further up the valley close to the stepping stones. These proposals are intended to eliminate the continuing conflict between cars and pedestrians travelling between the car park and the road head at the Stepping Stones. Visitors would be encouraged to use the roadway as the main footpath into the valley lessening the use of the footpath on the eastern bank of the river. The latter is being adversely affected by river erosion. There have been two accidents resulting in individuals seeking to take the highway authority to court for compensation. (Should the latter succeed, there would be pressure to surface the footpath, with adverse affects on the appearance and nature conservation interest of the area). Relocating the footbridge would substantially reduce the use of the footpath on the eastern side, since access to the main car park would be much more difficult, although it would remain as an alternative route for longer distance walkers. The relocation would also reduce direct access to the hillside at Thorpe Cloud allowing the removal of the fencing.

There was considerable discussion as to whether the relocation of the footbridge was desirable, particularly in terms of the impact on the setting of the Stepping Stones. The Dovedale visitor management scheme is generally considered to be successful although there is no evidence available on its impact, either in terms of visitor numbers or the degree of use of the area.

White Peak Area

The party then travelled through the White Peak area to Monsal. En route the party passed the Tissington Trail, created along a disused railway line, which is used by walkers and cyclists. The National Park Authority operates a cycle hire facility on the Trail and elsewhere in the Park which now makes a small profit. However, the number of private cycles has risen to some 60 per cent of users.

Monyash, through which the party travelled, is one of three communities involved in the Integrated Rural Development programme run by the National Park Authority in the 1980s, with assistance from the European Commission and national agencies. Under the programme, each community developed their own proposals to enhance the village with a view to encouraging greater benefit from tourism as well as environmental and social benefits. Projects undertaken in Monyash included an extension to the village school, improvements to the village hall, new planting of ash trees, a children's playground, the conversion of underused buildings for self catering holiday accommodation and a village car park. Much of the work was undertaken by the community itself with financial assistance from the programme.

Arriving at the Monsal Trail, the party transferred to four wheel drive vehicles. The trail is used by walkers and for part of the route by cyclists and riders, although sections including tunnels are closed to the latter and bypassed by walkers.

Hathersage

The party then proceeded via Winnats Pass to Hathersage. The Pass was the location of a traffic initiative involving its closure during summer weekends, which had to be discontinued when the main alternative route was itself closed as a result of land slips.

At Hathersage, the party received a briefing on the Peak Tourism Partnership from *Chris Lewis*, Director. The Partnership had been set up following the Tourism Task Force report, and included eight local authorities, Severn Trent Water plc, Center Parcs, the Tourist Board and other agencies. It had core funding for three years of £100,000 a year.

Its objectives are to:

Encourage sustainable tourism and visitor management;

Raise the contribution which tourism makes to the environment; and

Give further impetus to joint work between the interested partners.

Its work has focused on several specific elements:

Visitor management schemes had been instigated at the Roaches and in the Castleton/Edale/Hope area. The latter scheme has very much involved local communities, through working groups and workshops, to agree the main priorities and actions required.

The Castelton strategy includes:

Traffic management and calming measures;

Park and ride;

The development of the footpath network;

Training for local people; and

A new visitor information centre.

The park and ride scheme has made use of the Hope Valley Rail Line, with a pilot project involving increasing frequency of Sunday services, linked bus services and guided walks and farm visits from the stations in the area. Monitoring surveys indicated that some 80 per cent of the people using the service would otherwise have come by car (saving an estimated 1,200 car visits to the valley.) About 6,000 people used the service out of approximately 2.5 million visitors.

The Tourism Heritage Trust is intended to finance a central co-ordinator to raise and distribute moneys raised from visitors and other interested parties for environmental enhancement projects. Two pilot fund raising schemes have been instigated. A number of hotels were seeking to raise money from voluntary contributions from their customers; and contributions were also being collected at three car parks in the area using additional ticket machines in the car parks. These issued a support sticker for any contributions received.

The amounts raised as of March 1995 were small—the pilot schemes had only been in operation for a few months—but the Partnership was hopeful of raising significant amounts from these and other schemes.

Some 125 projects had been identified by the Partnership, which is now looking to put together a £1.5 million package with funding from the EU Objective 5(b) programme. The Partnership had been able to complement the work of the individual bodies; it had brought together a wide range of bodies which did not always work together; it had adopted a topic based focus; and it had been able to take an independent stance. However, three years was not long enough to ensure success.

Following the briefing, the Peak District National Park Authority hosted dinner for the Committee at Losehill Hall, the National Park Study Centre. *Councillor Martin Doughty,* Chairman of the National Park Authority and *Chris Harrison,* the National Park Officer, briefed the Committee on the organisation, changing role and circumstances of the National Park and led an informal discussion on outstanding issues affecting it.

THURSDAY 8 MARCH

Derwent Valley

The Committee travelled to the Derwent Valley to visit the visitor management scheme in operation there. En route the party drove through Bamford village and past the Ladybower Reservoir. As part of a new initiative, the National Park Authority was operating a bus service from Bamford station to Fairholme in the Derwent Valley at weekends, as an alternative to travelling by car. The Heatherdene car park at Ladybower was to be extended to allow the reduction of car parking on the road alongside the reservoir.

At Fairholme visitor centre, *Ken Parker* outlined the history of the Derwent Valley Visitor Management scheme and current developments. In 1974, the Water Authorities were given the duty of providing for recreational use on their holdings. At that time, the Derwent Valley, while attracting a considerable number of visitors, only had one small car park and very poor toilet facilities. After five years of "shuttle diplomacy" between the National Park, the Water Authority and the Forestry Commission (a major land owner in the valley), a draft management plan was published in 1979. The plan proposed the closure of the road above Fairholmes resulting in objections from the Water Authority, CPRE and the parish council. However the Highway Authority was persuaded to proceed with the closure on summer Sundays, and the concept is now widely supported.

Closure has now been extended,with the road closed on weekends and bank holidays from Good Friday to the end of October and also on Sundays in the winter season. A bus service is operated hourly during the winter and every twenty minutes during the summer. Tickets cost 70p for those parking at Fairholmes, but only 40p for those travelling to the valley by public transport. The National Park subsidises the cost of the bus service. In addition to the road closure, car parking was extended in the valley with the main car park at Fairholmes having a capacity of 300 cars. Toilets were provided at Fairholmes together with an information room (which now attracts 70,000 visitors during the summer season), and a buffet outlet which is run by a concessionaire. The costs of the provision of the car park, and revenue costs, are met by Severn Trent Water plc with no car parking charge. A network of footpaths has been developed. A cycle hire outlet has also been provided with 100 cycles and a total of 13,000 hirings per year, covering its costs.

The visitor management scheme in the Valley has generally worked well although it has brought little benefit to local farmers, who are primarily tenants. However, the Valley has continued to increase in popularity resulting in increased congestion and roadside parking along the road to Fairholme. It has now been decided to take action to reduce the problem by declaring the road from the main road to Fairholme a clear way with no parking (enforceable by the police). An electronic road sign has also been installed on the road to indicate when the car park is full, together with a roundabout to allow traffic to turn and exit from the valley when this is the case. A decision had been taken not to extend car park capacity in the area. It was not known what would happen to traffic turned away from the Derwent Valley at peak periods.

The party was then taken up a forestry road to a Byway Open to All Traffic above the valley at Rowlees where there is a problem of four wheel drive vehicles causing excessive wear and damage to the surface. Problems had also been reported with groups of four wheel drive vehicles driving on and off road in the area during the night, causing nuisance and disturbance to farmers and their stock.

Pennine Way

The Committee then proceeded to Crowden where they were briefed by *Mike Rhodes*, the Pennine Way Footpath Officer, on the restoration work taking place on the Pennine Way and shown the air lift operation ferrying stone from Crowden. The Pennine Way is the premier national trail, but the number of walkers on the peat moorland sections has caused severe damage. In some cases the "path" was now some 20-30 metres wide.

The intention of the restoration work is to produce a sustainable walking surface capable of sustaining the walking pressure without damage to the adjoining area. There had now been several years of experimentation in the UK making use of new materials as well as more traditional techniques. Most of the former have not been successful, therefore a traditional approach had been adopted with regard to the Pennine Way whereby slabs of Pennine sandstone are "floated" on top of the peat in the eroded sections to provide a stable stone surface. Where the surface was stable, i.e., in areas where the overlying peat had been eroded to reveal the underlying sand and gritstone, no repair was necessary.

Since 1991, some 23 kilometres out of a total of 40 kilometres have been repaired on the Pennine Way within the Peak District National Park. Where paving is required, flagstones from disused mill buildings (mainly from the Bacup area) have been used. Some 1.5 kilometres are being laid this year with a further 4/5 kilometres planned over the next five years. The sections now being repaired were some way from a roadhead and therefore airlifting was the most cost effective way of transporting the slabs to the repair location. The average cost per lift is £15.

Members of the Committee were then carried by helicopter onto Dun Hill to look at damaged areas around the path. Unfortunately, snow effectively covered any sign of the underlying damage. At the landing site, a new fence had been erected across the open moor to separate two land holdings, on one of which the landowner had opted to join the Environmentally Sensitive Areas scheme. The scheme involves reducing stocking levels of sheep, and to prevent stock straying onto the land entered into the ESA scheme a stock proof fence has been erected. Overgrazing weakens the vegetation base which together with the acidic nature of the peat and the effect of trampling, causes the breakdown of the vegetation surface and consequent erosion of the exposed peat by rain. The Black Hill area was particularly badly affected.

The Committee then returned via the Strines area to Aldern House to receive formal evidence from the Peak District National Park Authority and the Peak Tourism Partnership.

ANNEX III

Note by Specialist Adviser

VISIT TO THE NEW FOREST AND POOLE HARBOUR AREA ON 21-22 MARCH 1995

BACKGROUND

Members of the Environment Committee visited the New Forest and Poole Harbour areas in relation to their Inquiry into the Environmental Impact of Leisure Activities. The party consisted of:

Mr Andrew Bennett (Chairman)
Mr Geoffrey Clifton-Brown
Mr John Denham
Helen Jackson
Mr Michael Stephen
Mr Roy Thomason

Ms Sarah Adams (Assistant Clerk)
Ms Melanie Sault (Secretary)
Mr Geoff Broom (Specialist Adviser)
Mr Roger Sidaway (Specialist Adviser)

TUESDAY 21 MARCH

The Committee travelled by rail to Brockenhurst where it met *Arthur Barlow,* Deputy Surveyor of the New Forest; *Roger Busby,* Regional Director, Forest Enterprise; *Anthony Climpson,* Tourism and Publicity Officer, New Forest District Council; and *Peter Impett,* New Forest Officer. The party then proceeded through the New Forest to Moors Valley Country Park.

Moors Valley

Tim Dixon, Head Warden and *Alan Brakewell,* Chief Executive of East Dorset District Council made an initial presentation in the Visitor Centre of Moors Valley Country Park. There is a joint management scheme for the Country Park (managed by East Dorset District Council) and the adjoining area of Ringwood Forest (managed by Forest Enterprise). Recreation facilities within the Country Park include a golf centre and driving range, picnic and play areas, coarse fishing in Moors Lake (with fishing facilities for disabled visitors) and a narrow gauge steam railway. Within the Forest, there is a network of forest walks, a play trail, a Tree Top Trail and bridleways. The facilities are busiest at the weekend as the main clientele consists of families with young children. It is estimated that half of the visitors to the Country Park also use the Forest. Many have a fear of getting lost within the plantations but are encouraged by the way-marking of paths. Three thousand visitors use the play trail on a busy Sunday. It is considered that the recreation attractions in Moors Valley have created a new market and it is unlikely that many visitors have been diverted from the New Forest. The net revenue is equally divided between the Council and Forest Enterprise. The Council estimates that its share of the revenue enables it to break even on current expenditure. Although dry conditions in the Spring and Summer frequently result in extreme fire danger conditions, this does not necessitate the area being closed to visitors.

The party toured the facilities including the Tree Top Trail.

The New Forest

The party then returned by coach through the New Forest to Lyndhurst, joined by *Graham Carter,* County Surveyors' Department, Hampshire County Council and *David Stagg,* a representative of the Court of Verderers. During the drive the Environmental Appraisal procedures undertaken by Forest Enterprise prior to clear-felling were described.

Mr Carter described the Highway Strategy for the New Forest. The strategy was approved by the County Council in 1989 and its primary purpose is to preserve and enhance the environment of this unique area which is visited by ten million people every year. Particular emphasis has been placed upon reducing the numbers of accidents to both people and forest stock animals (ponies, cattle, sheep and pigs). Roads in the Forest have been classified into a hierarchy and a 40 mph speed limit has been introduced on unfenced roads. On certain stretches the carriageway has been narrowed and passing places provided to restrict speed further. The restrictions are distinctively signed by constructing "gateways" at the main Forest entrances and by carriageway markings. The Strategy has been supported by an extensive publicity campaign. To date, the County Council has invested £300,000 in the Strategy through its Capital Programme.

An evaluation of a pilot scheme showed a significant reduction in traffic speed. Whereas previously approximately 80 per cent of traffic travelled at over 44 mph, now 80 per cent travels at under that speed. Personal accident injuries have been halved and animal deaths reduced by one-third. A driver attitude survey undertaken by the Transport Research Laboratory showed that the scheme was well accepted even though it causes inconvenience to drivers.

Despite the success of the Strategy, traffic pressures continue to grow and a working party of representatives from interested organisations has been formed to review the 1989 Strategy. The transportation package under consideration includes measures to: minimise congestion in the village of Lyndhurst; improve public transport to and within the Forest; alter junctions to restore the rural nature of the area and identify potential road closures.

Mr Barlow described the current review of recreation provision within the Forest. The purpose is to reconsider the location of car parks for day visitors, with the aim of reducing them below the present number of 141. Shrubs and undergrowth have been removed around certain car parks on the Rhinefield Drive to increase their visibility from the road and thereby reduce theft from parked cars. A report has been prepared on horse riding and the ways in which revenue might be raised to repair many heavily used routes, as many commercial stables currently use these routes free of charge. The provision of campsites is also under review, with the aim of improving facilities for campers, as ground conditions in many of the original locations have proved difficult to maintain to an acceptable standard. The income of £1.2 million from camping fees generates a surplus of £450,000 which is used to pay for environmental work in the open forest. However, the total net cost of this work is estimated to be £1.4 million, equivalent to 18p per visitor to the Forest.

Mr Barlow went on to describe the consultation procedures within the New Forest. Forest Enterprise is legally obliged to consult the Verderers on recreation provision and to compensate them for any loss of grazing income. The New Forest Consultative Panel meets six times a year and the Open

Forest Advisory Committee has a wide representation of local groups. A Recreation Users Advisory Committee was established earlier this year.

The party then proceeded to the Verderer's Court, Queens House, Lyndhurst and took oral evidence from the Forestry Commission, the New Forest District Council, Hampshire County Council and the managers of Moors Valley Country Park. The Committee stayed overnight at Studland.

WEDNESDAY 22 MARCH

Studland and Purbeck

The Committee travelled to the National Trust Visitor Centre at Knoll, Studland.

David Evans, Poole Heritage Committee, described the visitor pressures in Purbeck, which attracts similar levels of use to the New Forest. Tourist demand is changing, with a decline in the numbers of holidaymakers—which has affected the resort of Swanage—and an increase in day visitors from the growing conurbation of Bournemouth and Poole. While visitor levels during the peak summer months have remained stable, off-peak use at other times of the year has increased.

Road traffic pressures have become particularly acute within Studland as access is limited to the A351 road from Wareham to Corfe and the ferry from Sandbanks to South Haven Point. The Heritage Committee has been working in partnership with the local community to prepare an integrated traffic solution. This will feature a park and ride scheme centred on the re-opening of the Wareham-Swanage railway and the building of a new railway station.

Geoff Hann, National Trust, stated that the Trust acquired the Studland Estate from the Banks family in 1982. This includes the heathland area which is designated as a National Nature Reserve and Studland Beach which attracts 20,000 visitors on a peak summer day. The slipway provides an important access point for water sports and the Trust has observed an increase in out-of-season walking. Horse riding is permitted on Studland Estate during the winter. The car park contains 2,200 spaces but overflow parking is required on seven or eight days a year, at which time 3,500 cars may be accommodated within the parking areas and up to 200 cars are parked illegally on neighbouring road verges. At these times there are acute pressures of litter, dogs, lost children and road congestion. This situation was inherited by the Trust and the need to manage recreation pressures at such a high density is unusual on Trust properties.

Although the Trust policy is to encourage people to take their litter home, litter removal is a major problem. After public holidays such as Easter, it takes two weeks to clear up the beach. Trust staff collect 12 tons of litter per week and £30,000 a year is spent on emptying bins. Litter is also brought in from the sea by boats using Poole Harbour or mooring off Studland Beach. There is a major pollution factor from boats when up to 400 yachts anchor overnight in Studland Bay.

Paths are formed through the dunes following desire lines and it has become necessary to discourage people from using them by fencing. Whereas a heavy palisade would appear too restrictive and would be broken by vandals, a basic two strand wire is sufficient to discourage most people. Ditches have been created to stop four-wheel drive vehicles getting onto the heath and motor cycling has been effectively stopped by taking a hard line and prosecuting offenders, who are invariably local. The Trust has greater problems with motor cycling in urban fringe areas such as Upton Heath and some provision for motor sports has been made at Ringwood.

There is a major problem of dogs fouling the beach but it is impossible to ban dogs because the South West Coastal footpath, which is a public right of way, runs along the entire length of the beach. This is not a problem in winter and in summer rangers ask dog owners to keep their dogs on a lead. Although there is a by-law requirement that pooper-scoopers should be used, this is unenforceable and this form of pollution gives rise to the highest number of complaints from the public. With 200 dogs on the beach each day, it is impossible to get the names and addresses of offending dog owners who are not usually local. The Trust has considered providing free scoops and separate bins but has been deterred by the cost of £80–£100 per bin.

Income at Knoll/Studland amounts to £170,000 a year which in part subsidises the maintenance of Corfe Castle and Kingston Lacey House. The Trust has attempted to provide low cost houses for local people via a housing association. Council house tenants exercised their right to buy but have resold the houses as holiday homes, thereby decreasing the number of houses available for local people. The National Trust encourages alternative enterprises on tenant farms.

The Committee travelled to South Haven Beach where a Royal Marine landing craft provided transport to the National Trust Pier on Brownsea Island. The Committee met representatives of the Poole Harbour Commissioners and Poole Borough Council and transferred to a passenger launch to tour Poole Harbour and discuss the aquatic management plan.

One of the largest natural features of its kind, the harbour contains 4,000 hectares (10,000 acres) of water, mudflat and several picturesque islands. The developed northern shore of Poole Borough contrasts with the undeveloped natural areas of the southern shore, which is of high conservation value. Poole has been a commercial port for 2,000 years and now handles roll-on/roll-off cross channel ferries, cruise vessels and conventional cargo services. Off-shore drilling operations by oil and gas companies are supported by the comprehensive services offered by the Port.

Following an Act of Parliament in 1895, the care of the harbour is entrusted to the Poole Harbour Commissioners whose duties are to "conserve, regulate and improve" the port and harbour of Poole. This they do with funds generated from the dues of shipping, cargo handling and passenger traffic. Thus the Commissioners seek to balance a viable commercial port, environmental protection and a thriving leisure industry. Poole was one of the first harbours in the UK to initiate a management policy in consultation with other statutory bodies (particularly English Nature) by establishing the Poole Harbour Steering Group. The Management Policy Document, published in 1988, was amended in 1991 and sets out the planning policies around the shorelines of the harbour. This is now complemented by a draft Aquatic Management Plan issued as a consultation draft in 1994 which identified potential conflicts of activities on the water areas of the harbour as well as the issues of safety and ecological protection. For many years the Commissioners designated the southern and western sections of the harbour as areas for quiet recreation to protect wildlife. The main controls on leisure activity introduced in the 1994 plan are the allocation of activity zones for high speed sports and the introduction of a by-law to restrict power-driven craft to a 10 knots speed limit throughout most of the harbour.

The Steering Group instigated two studies in 1994 which provide base line data and verify or augment statements made in the draft plan. A project officer and consultants were appointed to conduct an aerial survey of recreational use of the harbour and a questionnaire survey of recreational users. The RSPB conducted a survey of bird life in the Harbour area and the impacts of commercial and recreational activities upon their breeding success. The Project Officer also supervised a detailed consultation exercise on the draft Plan.

The recreation activity survey found that visitors to Poole Harbour are generally content with the current level of use and support the enforcement of the by-laws. Their main concern was the lack of shore-side facilities such as showers and parking for cars and trailers. While the majority of participants in the "traditional" water sports, such as sailing, motor boating and water skiing, had been involved in their sport for over ten years, most participants in windsurfing and jet skiing had only taken them up within the last two to three years. Club membership was most popular amongst members of the sailing fraternity. In all other water sports the majority of participants were not club members. While the majority of respondents said that other activities did not affect their enjoyment of their own sport, members of the sailing fraternity said that other activities did cause irritation.

It was estimated from the aerial survey that the mean number of boats was approximately 2,400 craft on the water with 1,200 in the wet berths provided by the major marinas. At peak periods, the total reached some 4,200, of which about a third were in the marinas. On average, about 11 per cent of the craft present in the harbour were moving, rather than moored, berthed or at anchor. This proportion increased slightly on public holidays and Sundays. These figures are substantially lower than those previously available, which may indicate that current harbour usage is lower than previously or that the former estimates were inaccurate.

The breeding bird survey found that the populations of each key breeding species in 1994 compared favourably with previous estimates. Only two species, the Sandwich tern and the Mediterranean gull had experienced a decline in breeding populations since the mid-1980s. However, it is not possible to determine whether this represents a long-term trend or to suggest the possible causes of this apparent decline. Higher numbers of breeding redshank were recorded than in previous surveys, confirming the regional importance of Poole Harbour for this species. Few incidents of disturbance to breeding birds by recreational and commercial craft were recorded in this study. The main gull colonies are still subject to wilful disturbance through egg collecting which is potentially damaging to the small population of Mediterranean gulls. Very little disturbance to breeding redshank and shellduck was observed, and there is little to suggest that major conflict between breeding redshank and water-borne recreation is occurring at present. The breeding redshank appear to be concentrated in the most inaccessible, quiet, salt marsh areas of the harbour although other factors such as habitat suitability and grazing management are also linked to breeding density.

The consultation exercise revealed that there was widespread general support for the fundamental idea of managing the various activities which take place in Poole Harbour.

The party alighted at Town Quay Poole where the Commissioners hosted a buffet lunch before the Committee was transferred by coach to Poole Civic Centre where it took formal evidence from the National Trust, Dorset County Council, Poole Harbour Commissioners, Purbeck Heritage Committee and the British Water Ski Federation. The Committee returned to London by train.

ANNEX IV

Note by Specialist Adviser

VISIT TO THE VELUWE NATIONAL LANDSCAPE, THE NETHERLANDS ON 28 APRIL 1995

BACKGROUND

The Environment Committeee visited De Hoge Veluwe National Park in the Netherlands as part of its inquiry into the Environmental Impact of Leisure Activities. The party consisted of:

Mr Andrew Bennett
Mr Robert Ainsworth
Mr Geoffrey Clifton-Brown
Mr Harold Elletson
Helen Jackson
Mr Bill Olner
Mr Roy Thomason

Mr Steve Priestley (Clerk)
Mr Roger Sidaway (Specialist Adviser)

NATIONAL PARKS AND NATIONAL LANDSCAPES

The Netherlands applies two different designations to rural areas of recognised conservation value: National Landscapes and National Parks. National Landscapes are extensive areas, in both public and private ownership, which have been designated because of their scenic quality and cultural value. A range of different land use functions is permitted. Thus they are roughly equivalent to Areas of Outstanding Natural Beauty in England and Wales. National Parks are smaller areas managed for conservation, environmental education, recreation and research, usually by one or more public bodies, e.g., Staatsbosbeheer (the Dutch forest service which manages forests and nature reserves) or by non-governmental trusts, e.g., Naturemonumenten (which principally manages nature reserves). Eight National Parks have been established and 13 proposed in the Netherlands: these range between 1,200 and 7,000 hectares in size.

Although "National Park" is now an official designation administered by the Ministry of Agriculture, Nature Management and Fisheries, many of the areas have been managed for more than 60 years by private foundations and have always used the title National Park.

INTRODUCTION TO THE VELUWE

The Veluwe is a National Landscape within the province of Gelderland, bordered by the Velumerandmeren (a lake on the edge of the reclaimed polders) to the north, the rivers Ijssel and Rhine to the east and south and the provincial border with Utrecht to the west. The hilly landscape, formed during the ice age, is an area of high ecological value which is also attractive for recreation. The Veluwe is the largest of the National Landscapes in the Netherlands covering 100,000 hectares

(250,000 acres). It has a distinctive character compared to the rest of the Netherlands, as 90 per cent of the area is forest or heath with very little arable land.

Initial Presentation of Evidence by Jan-Wilem Calicher, Head of the National Park Planning Office for Gelderland Province

THE IMPLEMENTATION OF NATIONAL LANDSCAPE POLICY

Within the three tiered structure of government in the Netherlands, the role of the *province* is to interpret *national government* policy strategically. The provincial strategy is then is given legal force in the local plan of the *municipality* (district council). A previously centralised system of planning has been changed to allow for local public participation.

Following the principles of "functional planning", different categories of land use (functions) are either segregated or concentrated in one place. The purpose of the National Landscape designation is to improve and maintain the environmental quality of the area, and the remit that has been handed down to the provincial government is to:

(a) Create a system of recreational zoning;

(b) Remove excess motorised traffic; and

(c) Improve habitats for wildlife.

The intention is to maintain and integrate the existing functions, including military use which can be concentrated into certain areas but not removed.

Master planning follows three stages: to analyse each function, to devise proposals to meet the objectives of the plan and to execute these proposals. The plan for the Veluwe is now in the third stage and the provincial government is currently seeking resources to execute the proposals.

The planning process was illustrated with reference to two related maps: a zoning map showing different intensities of recreational use and a "functions map" which showed the different types of forest and wildlife areas.

LAND USE FUNCTIONS

Forestry

There are 60,000 hectares of forest in the Veluwe and the policy is gradually to replace pine plantations with broad-leaved forest. This is a slow process: forestry in the Netherlands is not profitable and is conducted for social benefit. Home production provides for 8 per cent of timber needs and of that, 80 per cent comes from the Veluwe.

Of the total woodland area, 50 to 60 per cent is privately owned, 20 per cent is owned by Staatsbosbeheer and 20 per cent by Naturemonumenten and the Provincial Landscape Trusts. Dutch forest law obliges private owners to replant trees after felling to maintain the forest. In return for a woodland management grant of 130 guilders per hectare, private woodland owners have to provide for nature conservation and public access.

Agriculture

Although this is not a major land use in the Veluwe it is still of economic importance. The major conservation issue is to reduce nitrate pollution by burying slurry from intensively reared cattle.

Military use

This has taken place in the area for the last 100 years and now occupies about one-eighth of the area. Large army helicopters fly over the National Park and although there is no evidence to suggest wildlife is disturbed, visitors complain about aircraft noise.

Housing policies

Municipal policies restrict building to infilling and redevelopment rather than extending residential areas.

Motorways

A north-south motorway (A9) planned between Arnhem and Zwolle was diverted around the Veluwe when permission was refused for the motorway to be built through the royal estates to the north-west of Apeldoorn. Sections of the motorway between Arnhem and Apeldoorn were excavated to a depth of 8 metres to allow the construction of "cerviducts" (wide overpasses) for wildlife. Surveys of footprints show how successful this policy has been in encouraging deer to cross the motorway, which is fenced along its length.

Nature areas

Much of the Veluwe heathland is maintained to protect undisturbed areas for red deer and other large mammals. The Veluwe provides important wildlife habitats, including the only habitat for red deer in the Netherlands. There is a population of about 1,200 red deer and the aim is to remove the internal fences within the area so that the deer have free movement through the area.

Wild boar, badgers, foxes, mouflon and other mammals live in the forest. As there are no natural predators, surplus animals are culled by private owners who hold shooting rights. Some private owners also breed game for hunting. There is some debate about culling as the public assume this is hunting in disguise. Within the Hoge Veluwe National Park culling is undertaken by keepers, with some stalking for private clients.

As well as deer grazing, ponies and highland cattle are used to manage vegetation. Most of the wildlife, such as red deer and wild boar, were reintroduced. The natural inclination of wildlife within the area would be to move down to the river plain and water meadows to graze, but as these areas are no longer accessible, the population is not in a natural balance and has to be fed. The 2,500 wild boar on the Veluwe are enclosed by fencing as they do considerable damage to farm crops.

Recreation

Tourist accommodation, including many campsites, is mainly provided in local villages. No new tourist development has been allowed but there is a process of redevelopment and upgrading of existing facilities. Horse riding is very popular along the southern border of the Veluwe. The potential for conflict with other users is reduced by physically segregating horses, cyclists and walkers on separate trails. Mountain bikers tend to go anywhere, making legal enforcement by the police difficult and the system works through social control.

Motorsports are accepted as a valid countryside activity. The policy is to site noisy activities close to motorways, away from residential areas, and to prohibit illegal use elsewhere. There are three or four such facilities for motorsports in the Netherlands, but only two or three locations for clay pigeon shooting, which is less popular than shooting in indoor ranges.

RECREATIONAL ZONING

A system of roads was laid out for harvesting timber from forests that were planted in the Veluwe in the second half of the nineteenth century and the first half of the twentieth century. These roads have been gradually been closed to cars over the last 20-30 years as part of the policy of recreational zoning. This policy was illustrated by considering the plans for the south-eastern part of the Veluwe, which includes the Veluwezoom and the Hoge Veluwe.

Recreation facilities are concentrated on the edge of this sector, close to the villages. As well as closing unpaved roads, parking facilities are provided and there is a trail system which allocates routes for cycles, walking and horse riding. In the so-called extensive recreation areas, peace and quiet is provided for people and animals. The key is maintaining certain public roads between the villages which are the "open arteries of social life".

PROVINCIAL TRAFFIC POLICY

The province aims to stimulate environmentally friendly mobility by developing public transport for recreation, and expanding cycling and hiking facilities. The provincial policy is to restrict traffic by temporary closure of roads; either seasonally, or during the hours of darkness, or during the week, but these measures are controversial because of the fear of losing tourism revenue. These restrictions would apply particularly within the nature areas and National Parks. The province commissioned research on recreational mobility in the Veluwe, the aim being to establish projects which would encourage tourists to use public transport, rather than relying on the restriction of car use.

NATIONAL PARKS

There are two National Parks within the Veluwe—De Hoge Veluwe (5,400 hectares) and De Veluwezoom (4,800 hectares). Although both are heathland, they differ in character. The *Hoge Veluwe* is fenced, charges for admission and contains visitor attractions such as the Kröller Müller art gallery and the St Hubertus Castle. It has been managed since 1935 by the Stichting de Hoge Veluwe, a private trust. The *Veluwezoom* is hilly with more panoramic views and does not charge for access. It has been managed since 1930 by Naturemonumenten.

TOUR OF THE VELUWEZOOM

The Veluwezoom lies to the north-east of Arnhem and attracts two million visitors a year, 80 per cent of whom travel by car or motorbike. With as many as 5,000 cars and motorbikes on a busy Sunday, traffic queues are common but only a small area of the Park is accessible by car. There are several small restaurants and campsites along the road from Arnhem, which passes through a mixed pine and beech forest. Parking is not allowed on the road verges in the forest, and parking tickets are issued by the local police.

The three principal roads from the south converge on an attractive hill called the "Posbank". With fine panoramic views and a restaurant, this area attracts visitors from a wide catchment to walk, cycle or even ski when there is snow. Most visitors stay at the Posbank for a relatively short time. The slopes in front of the viewpoint have been fenced to reduce the trampling of vegetation, which has been severe in this heavily used area.

Posbank was a national meeting point for motorbikers with several hundred meeting each Sunday. This deterred other visitors, and the noise could be heard well within the quieter "natural" areas. The landowners (Naturemonumenten) sought some restrictions on cars and motorbikes but in this case the roads are owned by the municipality of Rheden. As the number of complaints from local residents grew, the municipality proposed to close two of the three access roads to all motorised traffic (rather than single out motorbikes for restriction). A local protest group was formed in Rheden and their legal action against the proposals was successful. Nevertheless many local people favour some traffic restriction and the protest was partly about their being excluded from the planning discussions. Meanwhile the motorbikers have voluntarily moved to a more acceptable venue. Discussions on traffic restrictions have reached an impasse and it has proved more difficult to reduce traffic in the area than anyone had anticipated.

Initial Presentation of Evidence by Mr A J Snijders, Deputy Director, Hoge Veluwe National Park Foundation

HOGE VELUWE

The area is mainly forest (about 2,700 hectares) and heathland. Although the landscape is perceived to be natural, it is an "erosion landscape", formed as farmers removed and composted turf to improve the soil quality of their nearby land. The result is a very degraded soil but also a very rare habitat containing many species that do not occur anywhere else in the Netherlands. (Turf removal can no longer be used as a management technique because of high levels of cadmium and lead from air pollution.) Grass has encroached into the heathlands as nutrient levels have increased from nitrate pollution and acid rain. The levels of pollution have called into question the value of heather restoration projects in the Veluwe.

The Kröller Müller family began purchasing estates in the Hoge Veluwe from 1910 onwards. Their vision was to unify culture and nature for the common good, aiming to build a museum in the heart of a natural area. In 1935 when they could no longer maintain the estate, they gave their art collection to the government, which built an art gallery within the Hoge Veluwe. The Kröller Müllers then made over their estate to a foundation on condition that it perpetuated the family objectives and was open to the public.

The Hoge Veluwe is one of the few National Parks in the Netherlands which charges an entrance fee, covering entrance to the art gallery. This forms a vital source of independent revenue for the park foundation, which is keen to take responsibility for the area and not be subject to changes in government policy. The current entrance charges are 7.50 guilders for adults plus 7.50 guilders per car, with children admitted at half price. There are reductions for school parties but not for students or pensioners.

The museum gets 20 per cent of the income from admissions plus VAT; the VAT element is being decreased to 6.5 per cent because of the educational value of the facilities within the National Park. The park foundation owns all the commercial facilities, which are operated by concessions or contractors.

FENCING

There has been a continual dialogue with the province for the last 10 years about the ring fence. The advantages of fencing the park are seen to be that it:

— Controls visitor access;

— Protects vulnerable habitats within the park from outside influence;

— Keeps deer and other large mammals away from the popular visitor attractions in the centre of the park (the museum, visitor centre, restaurant and landscape garden);

— Helps the operation of the free white bicycle scheme.

WHITE BICYCLE SCHEME

White bikes were introduced into the National Park in 1973 as an experiment, taking the idea from the 1960s flower power movement in Amsterdam. Visitors can get on a bike at one point and leave it at another. Up to 6,000 bikes can be in use on a peak day, with park staff engaged in redistributing bikes to the most popular pick-up points. If anything, there are now too many cyclists using the area but it has become difficult to reduce the numbers because visitors expect to get a bike as part of their entrance fee. The scheme is costly to maintain but theft is not an issue—only 10 or 15 bikes are stolen each year.

The present number of visitors, about 700,000 per year, is considered to be too high and as a result current policy is to reduce attendance levels to about 600,000. However, this calculation is based on the estimated financial break-even point and is not an indication of the capacity of the facilities.

Question and Answer Session in the Rijzenberg Centre

QUESTIONS ON THE VELUWEZOOM (J W CALICHER)

Financial resources

In the early stages of the Veluwe plan, 90 per cent national government funding was available with 10 per cent being provided by the province. This has now fallen to a 50/50 split: 50 per cent from national government, 25 per cent from Gelderland and 25 per cent from municipalities and the private sector. The province has had to rephase expenditure as and when funding becomes available.

Footpath erosion is not a major issue. It only occurs on intensively used areas like Posbank. The general policy on footpaths is to concentrate use and to provide an appropriate surface.

Camping in the wild generally does not occur in the Netherlands because campsites are provided but camper vans do trespass and stay in the National Park overnight. There is no comparable provision to the "exempt organisations" provisions in British caravan and camping Acts. Recent legislation encourages farm camping, allowing up to five units per farm. There is some concern over the impacts of this scheme but because it requires considerable investment in toilet facilities, many farmers may not consider it worthwhile.

There is little pressure for *major leisure developments*. However, since forest land is worth 10,000 guilders a hectare compared to agricultural land at 50,000 guilders a hectare, pressures for new developments such as golf courses are exerted on forest land, with few developments on the more expensive agricultural land. Four golf courses have been constructed in the Veluwe over the last ten years. These were either granted permission because of existing rights or because of "democratic pressures within the municipality".

Further explanation of *zoning* illustrated how mass facilities were provided around the Veluwe, and how water sport facilities acted as honeypots. Asked whether this policy has reduced pressure on the Veluwe, Mr Calicher's reply was that it was more likely to have coped with any increase in visitor pressure rather than reduced pressure overall. The general trend was for more people to have more time and make more visits to the countryside. The major predictions were not for population growth but increased mobility. For example, it appears that some people were prepared to travel 60 kilometres from Amsterdam just to walk their dogs: this was discovered when stray dogs were caught and their owners were found to be from the city. There are regulations that require dogs to be kept on a leash— although areas have been provided around villages to allow dogs to run free, this amounts to no more than 80 hectares in the Veluwezoom.

Changing trends in recreational use

There has been an increase in activity holidays, walking and cycling. More people are taking several holidays each year in spring, summer and winter; indeed autumn is now the busiest season in the Hoge Veluwe. The "more active elderly" were coming more often but despite these pressures the zoning system works. As most people walk no further than 800 metres it is possible to be alone.

Long distance trails

The Dutch national network tends to go from village to village and campsite to campsite. Most people prefer to stay in hotels when they are walking; they are prepared to suffer by day but want some comfort at night. There is a small scheme which provides primitive camping for cyclists on the Veluwe and this is maintained by Staatsbosbeheer and private owners.

Publicity

No deliberate campaigns had been mounted to direct people to less sensitive areas, although the regular Veluwe bulletin tells people where problems or events are and they tend to respond.

Outstanding problems

Vandalism close to urban areas occurs in phases and is an insoluble problem. There is some trespassing on motorbikes into recreational areas, particularly by young people on mopeds. Theft from cars declined after a police campaign and this problem has been also been reduced by removing vegetation which screened car parks. The province had attempted to introduce a white bike rental scheme in the Veluwezoom, which they were prepared to subsidise, but at the time of the visit they could not operate it on a break-even basis.

The most difficult planning problem has proved to be the implementation of the policy, introduced in the 1970s, to reduce motorised traffic on public roads.

QUESTIONS ON THE HOGE VELUWE (A J SNIJDERS)

Balancing investment priorities

While there are always incentives to improve facilities and increase levels of use, managers had to ensure that they protected the natural resource. The park foundation was keen to invest in educational facilities: a recent example is the underground museum which has proved very popular with children.

Traffic management

Most people wanted to use their car to get to the centre of the National Park, and the park foundation could not afford to close the roads as this would affect their revenue. As many as 100,000 cars park in the centre—which illustrates the popularity of the central hub—compared to only 40,000 parked at the entrances. This does have advantages: by drawing people into the centre from each of the three entrances, it is possible to maintain the intervening areas as undisturbed zones (less so in the north because of St. Hubertus Castle). However, it is important to offer alternatives. The white bike scheme had started as a public relations stunt but it had been very successful. White bike stands are now provided at the car parks which were recently constructed at the park entrances.

Public transport is provided to the Park entrances, and a bus from Arnhem station runs through the park, providing an hourly service in the summer which reduces to two to three times a day during the weekends in the off peak season. There is also an hourly bus service from Otterloo to Hoenderloo along the public road, which runs on the northern boundary of the park and is connected to Apeldoorn. In 1994 about 40,000 visitors came to the National Park by bus—admittedly a small proportion of the 700,000 visitors. There are inherent problems because public transport has to be comfortable, frequent and without the need to change buses if people are to be tempted out of their cars. At the end of a long day, visitors do not want to wait a long time for a bus home and if this does happen, they come by car next time.

Peak pressures

The National Park foundation was keen to spread the season because of the peak pressures; each of the months of June, July and August attracted 100,000 visitors. However, research conducted by the Centre for Recreation and Leisure Studies of the Agricultural University at Wageningen questioned this strategy. It was found that people who came during the peak season accepted high levels of crowding without complaint, whereas visitors in April and October when it was much quieter were concerned that numbers might increase. The park foundation now recognise the needs of their different clientele and has abandoned the strategy of spreading the load. There appears to be little reason to be concerned about the impact of present levels of use on wildlife. The only populations that might be affected out of season are migrant birds, but there is no hard evidence on this potential impact. A scientific committee advises on park management, keeping it under scrutiny.

Zoning

The park foundation follows similar principles of zoning to the province, but on a much smaller scale. Single ownership eases management problems and it helps that there are no public roads through the area (because the Kröller Müllers had made a key purchase of the old road from Otterloo to Hoenderloo). There is an important distinction between purist and practical objectives. For the nature lovers, one more footstep is too much but if multiple objectives are being pursued the manager has to consider whether 5 per cent, 10 per cent, or 20 per cent damage is acceptable.

Income from forestry

The park's income from forestry is 100,000 guilders each year out of a 5 million budget. This revenue is not important compared to the value of the park as a nature reserve. Strict commercial objectives for forestry would conflict with conservation and would not be justified by the very low timber returns from such poor soils.

Distinctiveness

The initial vision and investment over the years has created a special quality within the park which makes it distinctive from other areas. It is this combination of the location, the museum, the white bike scheme and the hunting lodge which attracts so many people every year.

The role of the Hoge Veluwe in the new system of National Parks is under discussion. The park foundation wants to continue on the present basis and is not attracted by increased government funding and control, particularly as this would mean that it would have to prepare a management plan for approval by the government. Their system of accountability—through representatives of municipalities who are members of the park foundation—is not as democratic as that of "new" national parks (which encourage public involvement in planning) but is more democratic as than the management of state forests nearby.

ANNEX V

Note by Specialist Adviser

VISIT TO COTSWOLD WATER PARK, 9 MAY 1995

BACKGROUND

Members of the Environment Committee visited the Cotswold Water Park in relation to their inquiry into the Environmental Impact of Leisure Activities. The party consisted of:

Mr Geoffrey Clifton-Brown
Mr Michael Stephen
Mr Roy Thomason

Ms Sarah Adams (Assistant Clerk)
Mr Geoff Broom (Specialist Adviser)

The Committee assembled at Kemble Station and were met by *Cllr Margaret Brown,* Chairman Cotswold District Council, and *Cllr Sue Herdman,* Chair of the Cotswold Water Park Joint Committee, together with officers from the County and District Councils. En route to the Keynes Country Park, the party were briefed by *David Ball,* Assistant County Planning Officer, Gloucestershire County Council.

The Cotswold Water Park covers an area of some 25,000 acres between Poole Keynes in the west and Lechlade in the east. The River Thames flows through the area with the head of navigation at Lechlade, while the route of the derelict Thames and Severn Canal also passes through the Park. It contains over 100 lakes formed as a result of gravel working, with new lakes still being formed by the eight gravel extraction companies working in the area. Filling of the workings is discouraged except in special circumstances (eg alongside Fairford aerodrome) because of the need to avoid damage to the movement of water through the area. Because of differences in levels across the Water Park only limited linkages are possible between the various lakes.

The area is divided into three areas; a western area with some 80 lakes centred around Ashton Keynes; an eastern area between Fairford and Lechlade where most active workings are currently located, and a central linking area which is held as a strategic reserve. The great majority of the Park area is in private ownership.

The Park originated in the 1960s, to meet demand for a range of water sports from residents of the West Midlands and other areas. Since that time the growing national importance of the area for nature conservation has also been recognised, with the Park embracing water areas equivalent to the Broads, with high water quality.

In order to ensure a consistency of approach between the different local authorities involved, a Joint Committee was set up in 1969. Currently the Joint Committee has representatives from Gloucestershire and Wiltshire County Councils and Cotswold District and North Wiltshire District Councils together with representatives from English Nature and the Sports Council. The Committee has powers to raise money from its constituent authorities by agreement, and its purposes are to ensure a consistency of approach across the whole park area with regard to land use and management policies, to provide a forum for discussion and to manage the Keynes Country Park, established by the Committee in the western area.

The Committee has produced a strategy which adopts a zoning approach distinguishing between:

— Quiet Zones, with priority being given to protecting the residential amenities of settlements, emphasising low intensity uses and quiet enjoyment of the countryside. After-use of the gravel workings is primarily for nature conservation, although the provision of circular rights of way to allow access for quiet enjoyment is also sought;

— Low Intensity Recreation Zones, within which a range of recreation uses may be permitted provided that there is no significant creation of noise or traffic nuisance. Quiet water sports may be appropriate; and

— Water Sports, Recreation and Tourism Zones, within which medium to high intensity uses will be permitted provided there is adequate access. These zones are primarily located away from existing settlements and with good access to the spine road and/or other major routes.

The strategy is being incorporated within Local Plans as they are prepared by the District Councils. In order to assist in the future development and management of the Cotswold Water Park, a Cotswold Water Park Trust has been formed with representatives from the four local authorities, private sector nominees put forward by the local authorities, the local nature conservation trust, the National Rivers Authority, the local village group, recreation users and representatives from the gravel companies and from developers. The Trust will seek to raise funds including contributions from developers to take forward conservation and restoration projects in the Water Park area.

KEYNES COUNTRY PARK

The Committee proceeded to *Keynes Country Park* where the party was joined by *Barbara Miley*, Secretary of the Cotswold Water Park Villages Society, and other officers. *David Ryan-Ainslie*, Cotswold Water Park Liaison Officer, briefed the Committee on the Keynes Country Park which had been managed by the local authorities for over 20 years. The Country Park includes three lakes which take up most of the area of the Park since the gravel companies had generally attempted to work right up to the boundaries of their sites. One lake is managed as a local nature reserve by the Gloucestershire Trust for Nature Conservation, a second lake is used for boating and fishing activities, while the third includes an artificially constructed beach and is used for swimming. The latter was created to overcome the problems of unauthorised use of lakes for swimming, which apart from any pollution or disturbance to wildlife also posed considerable safety problems.

The main emphasis in the Keynes Country Park is on informal recreation and enjoyment, with more organised recreation being run by clubs and/or private sector interest on other sites within the Cotswold Water Park. An estimated 200,000 people visit the Country Park each year with up to 800 cars on site at any one time. The site offers the main parking facility in the Water Park, with additional public parking provided in smaller car parks sited along the spine road. The Joint Committee would like to see the private sector making similar provision in other areas of the Park to reduce the pressure on the Keynes Country Park.

FRIDAY ISLAND

The party then proceeded to Friday Island, a privately owned and operated site which is in a Quiet Zone because of its close location to Somerford Keynes. The site consists of two linked lakes, and over a 15 year period the owners have greatly enhanced the conservation value of the site by planting 37,000 trees (for which they received some grant assistance from the Forestry Commission) and establishing reed beds. The main commercial use is for corporate hospitality, including product launches and team building events. The owners also let one holiday cabin and grant fishing rights to a pike syndicate during the winter. The planning permission limits the number of people on site to a maximum of 300 except for a limited number of days when up to 2,000 people can be accommodated. The owners have purchased two electric launches which provide quiet and conservation-friendly trips on the lakes.

HOLIDAY PARKS

The party then travelled back towards Ashton Keynes along the spine road passing the site where planning permission had been won on appeal by Lakewoods for a Center Parcs style holiday village with up to 700 chalets. There had been strong local opposition on the grounds of both damage to conservation interests and noise and nuisance. *Mrs Miley* suggested that the impact of service lorries and the large number of visitors would be significant, while noise was already increasing as a result of planning permission being given for a light aircraft strip nearby (noise nuisance has also been a problem in the past with active gravel working and a major air force establishment at Fairford aerodrome). Lakewoods have announced that they are not intending to proceed with the development of the holiday village and the site is currently on offer.

Close to the Lakewoods site is Hoburnes Cotswold caravan site. This site was the first to be purchased and developed by a tourism operator following the completion of gravel working. The site includes central club facilities, a swimming pool, wooden chalets and 700 touring caravan and tent pitches. Although the site does include a small lake, there is little recreational use of the water area.

APPLICATION OF ZONING PRINCIPLE

The Group then visited one of five Watermark sites within the Park on Lake 14, where they were met by *Jeremy Paxton,* Managing Director of Watermark, the site manager and accompanying staff. The main principles pursued in connection with development of the Watermark sites were explained: all the sites are within zone C, within which priority is given to tourism/recreation use providing that it does not damage nature conservation interests.

The Lake 6 site was taken as an example. Development has been concentrated on the north bank. A mini-country park with interpretative facilities has been provided together with a number of second home lodges. Priority has been given to nature conservation interests on the south bank of the site; there is progressive zoning on the water area, with more intensive water recreation activities being concentrated at the northern end, an intermediate zone by a Quiet Zone at the centre of the lake, and the southern end. The steep banks of the gravel workings have been graded back to encourage paddling duck as well as diving duck species, while a footpath with bird hides has been constructed around the lake. Similar principles have been adopted at the Lake 16/17 site, with development being concentrated at one end of the site and nature conservation given priority at the opposite end.

In response to questions, *Kevin Field,* Principal Planning Officer, Cotswold District Council, indicated that within the Park as a whole, zoning policy is considered important in resolving conflicts between recreation, conservation and community interests. Major concerns centring around motorised water sports have been resolved by limiting the activities to certain lakes. On the zone B lakes there is some occasional conflict between boating and fishing.

The strategy also includes the provision of a rights of way network providing circular routes throughout all the zones. However, in the past, gravel extraction companies have not always been scrupulous in protecting or reinstating rights of way. Sites were also often worked up to the hedge line, limiting the scope for creating new links. Gravel companies are now taking a more responsible approach with regard to conservation and access issues.

Access to and within the Cotswold Water Park is generally good, via the A419 dual carriageway and the spine road originally constructed for gravel working. Access to most sites is therefore possible without passing through existing settlements.

WATERMARK DEVELOPMENT

Mr Paxton then spoke about the Watermark development. It is intended to develop some 500 lodges distributed over 5 locations within the Cotswold Water Park. Ground conditions for development are often difficult on filled land and/or land with unstable banks. Therefore development costs are high. The lodges are timber framed and clad, and deliberately painted in light, pastel colours, very different to the stone cottages of the local Cotswold vernacular. There is a club building on site for the second home owners and local residents who can become members. Most of the holiday homes are purchased by city dwellers and looked after and managed by Watermark. Purchasers are almost exclusively English, mainly as a result of the targeted marketing, but they are likely to look at the overseas market as the development progresses. Typical occupancy is around 35 per cent so there is potential for a secondary holiday letting service.

Watermark have a current application for a further site on Lake 16/17 for 58 lodges. The lake has an established sailing club but with poor club house facilities, which Watermark intend to improve substantially. The application has attracted opposition on three grounds, namely from:

— English Nature, who are concerned with the impact on overwintering wildfowl, although the Lake has a long established history of sailing activity. Negotiations are proceeding with English Nature to secure an acceptable design and management regime;

— Existing lodge owners on Lake 14 who object to the new lodges on the adjacent site, although landscaping measures will effectively reduce the impact of the new development in due time; and

— Local residents who are concerned with possible additional traffic into the village.

There has been strong support from existing sailing club members, and a number of local benefits would arise from the development. These include:

— Some 120 jobs across all the Watermark sites;

— Upgraded links for walking and cycling, as well as an extension of the bridle way network;

— Contribution to the hydrological survey being undertaken by the NRA;

— Additional public open space;

— An agreement that no further accommodation would be developed on the site;

— The existing SSSI status would be safeguarded;

— A contribution equivalent to 1 per cent of the capital cost of development to be made to the Cotswold Water Park Trust Fund.

Mrs Miley indicated that the local residents concerns' about the Watermark development included the density of development, the intrusion into the landscape, a concern that lodges would turn into permanent homes and the impact on wildlife.

Mr Field commented that a substantial amount of landscaping had been carried out, and that the flat landscape and hedgerow pattern ensured that any intrusion was very localised. The District Council had attached conditions to the planning permission and agreed a Section 106 agreement with the developer to ensure that the lodges did not become permanent dwellings. Thus the lodge could not be the purchaser's primary residence, and there were strict conditions on such matters as hanging out washing, which would either preempt their use as permanent homes or make it easy for the managers to identify any cases of attempted use for such purposes.

CANAL REDEVELOPMENT

The party then proceeded to Swindon station, passing over the derelict Thames and Severn Canal close to the junction of the spine road with the A419. There are currently proposals for major improvements to the junction which provide an opportunity to reopen the canal route by inserting a bridge over the line of the canal. Unfortunately there is no agreement as to who should be responsible for the cost of the exercise and the Department of Transport is resisting the bridge proposal. The reopening of the Thames and Severn Canal through to Lechlade together with the link, via a restored Wiltshire and Berkshire canal to the Kennet and Avon canal would provide an attractive circular route for canal holiday traffic.

ANNEX VI

Note by the Specialist Adviser

VISIT TO THE LAKE DISTRICT NATIONAL PARK ON 13-14 MAY 1995

BACKGROUND

The Environment Committee visited the Lake District National Park in relation to their inquiry into the Environmental Impact of Leisure Activities. The party consisted of:

Mr Andrew Bennett (Chairman)
Mr John Denham
Mr Den Dover
Mr Roy Thomason

Ms Sarah Adams (Assistant Clerk)
Mr Geoff Broom (Specialist Adviser)
Mr Roger Sidaway (Specialist Adviser)

SATURDAY 13 MAY

The Committee travelled by rail to Oxenholme where it met *Bob Cartwright*, Head of Park Management and *Gill Huggon*, External Relations Officer, Lake District National Park Authority. The party then travelled by mini-bus to the National Park Visitor Centre at Brockhole where it met *Peter Phizacklea*, Leader of the Labour Group, *Kath Atkinson*, Chairman of the Planning Policy Committee, *Michael Sewell*, Chairman of the Visitor Service Committee, *John Pattison*, Chief Planning Officer and *Tony Hill*, Windermere Lake Ranger.

Brockhole: Lunch and Briefing

Bob Cartwright outlined the geography of the National Park, which covers 855 square miles (2,292 square kilometres) and has a population of 41,000 people. It is estimated that 14 million visits are made to the National Park each year and this contributes £346 million to the local economy. Nearly 60 per cent of the land is in private ownership, 25 per cent is owned by the National Trust and the remainder by various other public bodies. The annual gross budget of the National Park Authority is £5.3 million which includes a supplementary grant from Central Government of £3.9 million. Thirty five per cent of the budget is spent on park management, 30 per cent on administration, 18 per cent on land use and planning and 16 per cent on visitor services.

The Environmentally Sensitive Area (ESA) scheme is changing farmers' attitudes to public access. There has been a 40 per cent take up of this voluntary scheme in the last two years incorporating 11 access agreements. However, large areas of the Lake District are common land and commoners are reluctant to agree to reduced stocking levels and cannot agree how ESA money would be divided between them. Public access has been unaffected in the Lake District by water privatisation. If anything, access has been enhanced by the creation of permissive paths, some of which have been dedicated as Public Rights of Way.

Michael Sewell stated that Brockhole is the Authority's major visitor centre, catering mainly for families and educational groups. Developed in 1969, it was the first visitor centre in any National Park. Set in 35 acres of gardens, bordering Windermere, it attracts 160,000 visitors per annum. The buildings consist of two lecture theatres and two study bases as well as three exhibition rooms, a shop and a cafe. Asked about publicity on public access, Mr Sewell stated that guidebooks and leaflets were proving to be more popular than Ordnance Survey maps which most people find difficult to read. Simple A4 sheets describing short walks were found to be the most popular of all.

The party then boarded a passenger launch to travel across Windermere.

Lake Windermere

John Pattison, Chief Planning Officer, described Windermere as England's largest lake which attracts most forms of water sport. Windermere has long suffered from excessive noise, excessive wash, and too much ignorant and/or irresponsible behaviour with consequent infringement of the enjoyment of others to the detriment of the Lake's character generally. In recent years, such problems have been accentuated by the increasing variety of fast craft. Eleven thousand registered craft use the Lake and there are 1000 moorings and jetties. The average number of boats on a summer Sunday reached its peak in 1977 at 1400 craft/day. Water skiing has increased steadily since the mid-1970s. In March 1989, the National Park Authority held a seminar at Brockhole which was attended by a wide range of organisations with an interest in the Lake. All present agreed that the problems on the Lake were such that additional measures were needed. The National Park Authority suggested a management agreement but this failed to reconcile the various users. Legal powers do not exist to make bylaws which would require boat users to have compulsory insurance or prevent them from exercising the public rights of navigation on the Lake. This also precluded the introduction of a comprehensive zoning scheme. The National Park Authority considered new legislation but it became clear that any perceived threat to the right of navigation would attract stiff opposition and jeopardise the successful passage of any Bill. Following appeals from several quarters for the National Park Authority not to delay much needed measures, the Board eventually decided that the appropriate way forward was to promote a bylaw for a single 10 mph speed limit over the whole Lake.

This proposal was the subject of a recent planning inquiry which lasted 14 weeks. It has become a national issue in which the National Park Authority has been supported by the Countryside Commission but opposed by the Sports Council and the British Water Ski Federation. The National Park Authority proposes that any bylaw should be introduced over a five-year period and that the Sports Council should find suitable areas for water skiing and power boating outside the National Park. At the inquiry, the British Water Ski Federation, backed by local water sport centres, claimed that the proposals would result in the loss of 600/750 jobs from four water ski instruction centres and other facilities. The National Park Authority considers that only 400 jobs are likely to be lost and that there are longer-term possibilities of jobs being created from the diversification of the tourist industry.

Tony Hill, Lake Ranger, described recreation management on Windermere. Four organisations have patrol boats on the lake providing a co-ordinated service. The *police* are responsible for law enforcement while the *National Rivers Authority* are concerned with water quality and have successfully reduced phosphate levels in lake water. *South Lakes District Council* owns the bed of the lake, part of the shoreline and the main public landing point at Ferry Nab. It manages moorings under contract to the National Park Authority, which in addition to being the planning authority is also responsible for boat registration and bylaw enforcement.

As well as enforcing the bylaws, the *Ranger Service* promotes public enjoyment and the conservation of wildlife. Each patrol boat is double manned and co-ordinated using a common radio frequency and computer records.

The National Park Authority obtains significant income from moorings fees (£1,000 per annum); launching fees from public slipways (£15 per day—private landowners with lake frontage have free access), and annual registration fees (£45 per boat).

The party landed at Bowness on Windermere.

Bowness on Windermere

John Pattison explained the pressures to develop leisure and recreation facilities at the tourist "honey pot" at Bowness. The resident population of 7,000 is supplemented by an influx of 20,000 summer visitors. Bowness is the largest tourist centre in the National Park. For many people their first visit to the Lakes is by coach: they take a boat trip, view the National Park from the Lake and have a meal before returning home. Holiday homes comprise 15 per cent of the local housing stock, compared to 4 per cent for the rest of Cumbria. There are six timeshare developments. Further housing development has not been permitted in the local plan, but buildings can be restored and extensions to hotels may be permitted as long as they are no larger than 10 per cent of the existing property. Traffic congestion is a problem at busy times. Carriageways have been redesigned and pavements widened to improve visitor enjoyment with the introduction of a privately-run road train.

Red Acre Ghyll, Langdale

The party then travelled to Langdale where it was met by *Charles Flanagan,* Regional Land Agent, National Trust and *Peter Davies,* Area Manager, Lake District National Park.

Charles Flanagan stated that the problems of footpath erosion were first noticed in the mid-seventies by the National Trust and work began in the 1980s using the Manpower Services Commission's Community Programme. The major erosion problems are on Helvellyn, Langdale and Borrowdale. The Trust and the National Park Authority have established an Uplands Path Group (which includes a representative from English Nature). The Group has agreed a Policy on Path Maintenance which incorporates a set of principles and techniques, following the British Mountaineering Council's principles of minimal intervention. The initial intervention is to improve drainage. Improvements to the wearing surface of a path are only made where necessary and these usually take the form of stone pitching using local materials, with English Nature's approval in certain cases. The Trust conducts an annual monitoring programme covering 100 paths using voluntary lengthsmen to monitor previous repairs and to assess priorities for further work. *Peter Davies* and *Charles Flanagan* are preparing a manual on footpath repair techniques.

Peter Davies outlined the annual footpath repair programme of the National Park Authority. Ninety paths have been identified for priority treatment over the next few years and the Authority is putting together a funding package which will include bids to the British Upland Footpath Trust. There are some variations in policies on footpath repairs. While the National Trust aims to restore all paths, the Park Authority is only undertaking repairs to paths below 1,500 feet above sea level.

The erosion in Red Acre Ghyll extends to 30 metres width in places. Attempts have been made to choose a more sustainable line than the present path which follows a "desire line" straight up the Ghyll. Although the route is not a public right of way, it is a popular path from Great Langdale to Pike O'Blisco; the Trust's view is that there is no alternative to remedial work in this case. A programme of repair and vegetation restoration has been jointly prepared by the National Park Authority and the National Trust and this has been the subject of a successful £30,000 bid for funding from the British Upland Footpath Trust. The work will be carried out by the National Trust's Langdale path repair team.

The party then travelled to the Langdale Hotel where it met *David Fairs,* Managing Director of the Langdale Leisure Timeshare Complex.

Tourism and Conservation Initiative

David Fairs explained the background to the Tourism and Conservation Initiative in which tourism and hotel operators are invited to finance conservation work. There are 12 pilot schemes covering woodland management, access and historic restoration projects. *Mr Fair's* company underwrites the National Trust's employment of a footpath worker in the Langdale path repair team. In only nine months, timeshare owners have contributed £6,000 towards the £10,000 that the company is guaranteeing towards the project. Hotel guests who get the same letter inviting contributions have showed less interest in the scheme. He considers that the appeal of the scheme to visitors who walk in the hills, as he does, is that funding is sought for a specific project. He also considers that day visitors contribute even less financially yet put more pressure on resources in the winter.

The timeshare complex was developed at Elterwater's former gunpowder works during the 1970s. The occupancy of apartments is very high (98 per cent) compared to 65 per cent occupancy of an hotel room. Its clientele tend to be environmentally sensitive people, aged 40 plus, with children. An adventure playground and trim trail have been installed. Prices for an apartment vary from £2,000 for life in February to £15,000 for life in August. While holiday villages can be sited anywhere, timeshare schemes depend on the local ambience of the National Park.

The party travelled to Kentmere via Elterwater, Ambleside, Windermere and Staveley.

Traffic management

En route, *Bob Cartwright* described proposals for traffic management, including parking restrictions and the reconstruction of roadside car parks around Elterwater Common. These proposals were favoured by the parish council but were opposed by the owner of the Britannia Inn.

A Traffic Management Initiative—jointly sponsored by the National Park Authority, Cumbria County Council and Cumbria Tourist Board—aims to make public transport more attractive and the use of the car less attractive, to give pedestrians priority in villages and to provide routes for cycling and walking. It would establish a hierarchy of roads from motorways to trunk and local distributor roads. He gave as a specific example: the proposal for a 40 mph speed limit on the Crook to Sawtry Ferry road. Minor roads would have a restriction of 20 mph and coaches would be prohibited by width restrictions. Extensive consultation on the proposals is planned, which will include parish councils and bus companies.

Kentmere—car parking

At Kentmere, the party met representatives of the Parish Council. Kentmere is a relatively quiet valley without hotels or shops, with few bed and breakfast premises, limited car parking and no public conveniences. Kentmere Horseshoe is a popular 14 mile walk around the valley. A survey in 1994 estimated that 98 per cent of visitors came to walk in the valley and 85 per cent to complete the Horseshoe. However, the dead end road in the valley is often heavily congested, particularly by indiscriminate parking near the Village Institute on bank holidays. Temporary use is made of a field at Kentmere under the 28-day planning exemption and this can accommodate up to 350 cars. Drivers are asked to make a donation to church funds. Plans are being developed with the Parish Council to improve signing, redesign existing car parking areas and extend a subsidised experimental bus service which was introduced in 1994. However, objections to a park and ride scheme have delayed the implementation of the proposals. A car park was planned at Staveley but residents objected and it may therefore have to be sited further away.

Garburn Road—off-road vehicles

The party also visited the Garburn Road, an historical trading route now suffering from increasing use by off-road vehicles. *Bob Cartwright* explained that although the Lake District suffered few problems compared to other National Parks, there has been a recent upturn in use by commercially-led convoys of four-wheel drive vehicles which have resulted in increasing complaints from parish councils. The National Park Authority's approach to this problem is to initiate discussions to see how it can be managed, and only if this fails will it press for traffic regulation orders. The Garburn Road is one of a limited number of sustainable routes in the Park which might be used by off-road vehicles in an environmentally sensitive way. *Bob Cartwright* has been meeting representatives of the Land

and Recreational Access group (LARA) and commercial operators to get a joint commitment to a code of practice which will deal with specific complaints and promote the acceptable use of certain routes. LARA has agreed to the principle of a hierarchy of routes even though many other lanes have legal rights of access for motor vehicles. The Group recognises the value of exercising a voluntary restraint on these routes to demonstrate its commitment to sustainable use. Local motoring clubs are offering to help repair damage caused by recreational vehicles. Voluntary restrictions which prevent use of these roads at night are also being considered.

Sunday 14 May

The party, accompanied by *Bob Cartwright* and *Gill Huggon* travelled by coach to Watendlath via Grasmere, Dunmail Rise and Keswick. *Mr Cartwright* pointed out the bus station site in Ambleside where agreement has now been reached on its redevelopment for shopping and offices, after considerable local opposition. Locals wished to retain the bus station use and were also concerned about the impact of additional shopping provision in Ambleside. However, the bus company no longer wished to operate from the site.

Mountain Bike Route

The party proceeded past Rydal Water. There is currently only one bridleway in the area which concentrates mountain biking activity. The National Park is working with the National Trust and the British Mountain Biking Federation to identify some additional routes in order to spread the load. Originally there had been some concern about mountain biking but this had been greatly ameliorated by consultation with the British Mountain Biking Federation and the 27 commercial bike hire operators in the Park, to agree on recommended and preferred routes which are signed to encourage use by mountain bikers.

Mr Cartwright pointed out the provision of an off-road footpath on National Park Authority land at White Moss to take walkers off the carriageway, which is narrow and enclosed by stone walls.

Grasmere—coach park

The party then briefly visited the extended car and coach park at the south end of Grasmere village. The village had a problem with traffic congestion caused by slow-moving coaches. The solution has been to create a dedicated coach park at the southern end of the village for up to 20 cars and 10 coaches separate from the existing car park area, coupled with the introduction of a coach ban in the centre of the village which prevents through coach traffic. Service buses and coaches seeking access to hotels in Grasmere are exempted from the ban.

There had been vociferous opposition from the Friends of the Lake District and from commercial operators at the northern end of the village who were concerned with loss of trade. However the National Park Information Centre is also located at the northern end and has not reported any decline in visitor numbers. A footpath link to the northern end, together with an information board at the southern car park, will offset any potential reduction of coach visitors to the northern end. It was also noted that there are other car parks in the village including one provided by the National Park Authority at the northern approach.

The capital cost of the coach park extension has been some £27,500 while management costs of around £2,000-£3,000 are anticipated. The land is leased from the local sports club at a cost of £4,000 a year plus 6 per cent of the overall income. The National Park Authority has built a new stone wall to assist in reducing the visual impact of the car and coach park. The 10 coach and 48 car park spaces are anticipated to generate some £30,000 income per year. The scheme has been operating since Easter and has been very successful so far, with car parking receipts some 75 per cent above the forecast profile.

Thirlmere

The group then proceeded towards Keswick passing Thirlmere. The latter had been owned by Manchester Corporation as a water supply, which had allowed access to the open fells but not to the woodland around the lake itself. The lake is now owned by North West Water who since privatisation have been much more relaxed about access to the woodland area. The Water Company also fund the cost of a National Park ranger for the area at a cost of £30,000 a year and have contributed a further £50,000 over two years towards the cost of rights of way repairs on Helvellyn. Erosion on the western approach to the latter has worsened considerably after the opening of a new car park at the Swirls by North West Water some years ago. Numbers using the path now average around 1,000 a day during the season with up to 1,500-2,000 on a peak day, although not all walk to the top. North West Water have also developed a lakeside path and discussions are taking place with regard to identifying a route for the Kendal/Keswick cycle route.

Arboth Fell to the west of Thirlmere has been designated as an SSSI, and is within the Lakes Environmentally Sensitive Area. Given the long tradition of open access to the fells the National Park Authority has resisted fencing there. However on Arboth, a case has arisen of one landowner entering into an agreement on stocking rates, but with his neighbour declining to participate. The Park Authority therefore agreed to the provision of a fence for the ten year period of the agreement.

Derwentwater Plan

At Surprise View at Watendlath, the party was met by *Mike Roulston,* the National Trust Warden for Borrowdale and *Martin Norris,* the National Park Authority's Area Manager. *Martin Norris* briefed the group on the Derwentwater Management Plan which encompasses the lake and lakeshore bounded by the road system. (Management plans have been produced for all the major lakes in the National Park). A document has been published for consultation with the National Rivers Authority, National Trust, local and parish councils and user groups.

The objectives of the Derwentwater Plan are to preserve the landscape and nature conservation interests while also encouraging appropriate recreational use, eg walking, picnicking and canoeing. Derwentwater ranks with Ullswater behind Windermere and Coniston in terms of intensity of use with up to 200 craft on the water on a busy weekend. English Nature is also considering designating the Lake as a SSSI, and the Lake has a significant angling interest as home to the "vendace." The main issues are:

— Erosion leading to the creation of bare land as a result of people pressure. Between 1982 and 1992, it is estimated that there has been an increase of 20 per cent in pedestrian use around the lake shore;

— Boating pressure; and

— Live baiting for pike during the winter season which can upset the ecological balance to the detriment of indigenous fish species.

A 10 mph speed limit has been imposed on the Lake. There has been no major problem of people subsequently breaking the speed limit. The National Park Authority does not control all the launch points but the two main commercial launch points control boats going onto the water. There is, however, access through a camp site where occasional incidents had arisen with jet skis. Safety cover on the Lake is primarily provided by the private ferry service supplemented by the occasional use of a National Park launch. There is also a problem with cycling since although there are no physical barriers, there is no legal right of way for cyclists. There are proposals to produce a visitor information leaflet for the Lake and for a voluntary ban on the use of the Great Bay area to provide a refuge area for overwintering wild fowl.

National Trust

Mike Roulston spoke briefly about the National Trusts' role in the Park. The Trust owns some 150,000 acres, about a quarter of the total area, as well as 88 working farms and 250 cottages, all of which are let to local people. As far as possible it is the Trust's policy to allow access to its land. He was responsible for the Borrowdale area covering some 25,000 acres owned by the Trust.

The main pressures affecting the area which arise from tourism include:

— Traffic pressures and congestion, with the public reluctant to leave their cars;

— User pressure on gates and stiles;

— Litter;

— Abuse and erosion of popular areas;

— Conflict with local/retired residents and farmers regarding nuisance and costs such as sheep worrying, wall and fence damage or over the location of car parks for a park and ride scheme; and

— Conflicts over housing with holiday homes and the pricing of local purchasers out of the marketplace, leading in extreme situations to the loss of local schools and shops.

On the other hand, visitors also bring benefits in terms of additional spending in the area. A local school raises around £3,000 from a raffle largely supported by visitors. The Trust encourages its tenants to take advantage of the opportunities to take in Bed and Breakfast guests, and has assisted tenants to put in central heating to enhance the operation. They have also encouraged small camp sites on farms. Visitors also contribute through the voluntary collecting boxes installed in eight cairns in the valley with an average contribution of £300 per year.

The National Trust manage four 4-man footpath teams in the park to maintain and restore footpaths on their land at an annual cost of £240,000, which includes the cost of a vehicle for each team.

As an experiment they intend to operate a park and ride scheme to Watendlath from Keswick on Sundays in the summer although traffic restrictions on the narrow valley road are opposed by local residents. The National Trust is running four 16-seat buses providing tours in the Lake District as part of the celebration of their centenary year, and it will have one such bus available for the park and ride service on Sundays. The route will involve a 45 minute journey each way. There will be no restriction on car parking in the valley when the service is running. A local bus company is proposing to run a rival service in competition.

Keswick

The group boarded a ferry launch from Ashness, landing in Keswick, and walked from the lakeside to the National Park Information Centre in the town. At the Centre, the party were met by *Mike Walker,* Manager of Keswick Tourist Information Centre, and his staff. He outlined the main services offered by the Centre. These include:

— A weatherline providing weather forecasts for those walking and climbing on the fells. It receives around 4,000 calls a day using 12 telephone lines. During the winter, a ranger goes up on the fells to record the weather conditions rather than just relying on forecasts. The calls have been retained on the local telephone network rather than the more expensive 0898 lines. Following earlier sponsorship by Cadburys, the service is now supported by Glaxo who have provided £25,000 for equipment and £40,000 per year for three years to run the service;

— The Camping Barn network within the National Park. There are 11 barns in the network charging £3 per night for basic accommodation in adapted barns offering a water supply, sleeping platform and cooking area. Toilet facilities using septic tanks are provided by the landowner. The network recorded 15,500 bednights last year. The Centre acts as the booking centre for the barns which are used 50 per cent by groups and 50 per cent by individuals. Each barn can accommodate up to 12 people and can be booked on an exclusive basis. Bookings can only be made through the Centre, which charges a commission of 12 per cent for the service;

— Greenside hostel on Helvellyn, providing slightly better standard accommodation for up to 18 people. The hostel is owned by the National Park Authority and charges are lower for youth users;

— A "bureau de change" service operated on an all-week basis, with most of the business taking place at weekends. They charge a flat fee of £2.50 and no commission, and have access to a FORCHEQUE scheme whereby visitors can cash cheques on their home bank. Some £51,500 had been changed so far in 1995;

— The provision of information such as mountain bike advice and leaflets, timetables for buses and launches; and

— The sale of books, guides and miscellaneous souvenirs produced by the National Park Authority.

This income offsets running costs, resulting in a net overall cost of 2p per visitor.

Compared with the Bowness centre, the Keswick centre deals mainly with walkers and active countryside users. There is a separate Tourist Information Centre operated by the local authority in the Moot Hall which focuses on standard tourist services such as bed booking and accommodation advice.

Blencathra

The group then drove to Blencathra Field Centre via the A66. There has been pressure to dual the A66 to improve access to the west coast. This is being resisted.

In discussion *Bob Cartwright* indicated that the National Park considered a number of footpath restoration options including stone pitching, diversion, reseeding, and temporary fencing. The National Trust was more likely to choose stone pitching as a preferred option. Car parking was also discussed. The National Park Authority have some 27 car parks in the Park. No charge is levied on the more remote sites.

At Blencathra, the group was met by *Martin McTernan,* the deputy warden. Having admired the panoramic mosaic made by local school children, the Committee was briefed on the work of the Field Studies Council and the Blencathra centre. The Field Studies Council was set up in 1943 and now runs 11 centres in England and Wales largely in leased buildings. The centres offer field study facilities for school children and adults although unlike many other centres they do not provide for outdoor activities. Courses are mainly focused on biology and geography; they remain the leader in the "A" level market. Adults used to be a major market although over recent years there has been considerable competition from universities, independent schools and even hotel groups. The Council not only offer environmental education but also undertake environmental research and most of their centres hold detailed records on changes in their areas dating back 20 years. They have recently been involved in transferring expertise to Eastern Europe, where there is a dearth of environmental education.

Blencathra was originally developed as a TB hospital, which finally closed in 1975. The National Park acquired it and ran it as a hostel until 1991. In that year the National Park and the Field Studies Council agreed on a joint project substantially to redevelop the site as a field studies centre. The centre has now been refurbished and redeveloped at a cost of over £750,000 (of which £250,000 has been raised on appeal) and opened in April 1995. The charges average £20 B & B plus £10 tuition fees per day per student. They are intended to cover costs and make a small contribution to the central costs of the Field Studies Council. Children come from mainly urban backgrounds and usually know little about the countryside environment. By contrast, adults are normally strong environmentalists. Many come from London and the South East, and courses focus on such aspects as transport, visitor conflicts, footpath management and upland farming. Farms used for educational visits receive a small fee. Staff avoid using questionnaires due to adverse reactions from local people in other areas who resented being the subjects of frequent surveys.

Ullswater

Following lunch, the Committee proceeded to Ullswater where it was briefed on the management plan. The lake is heavily used, with Pooley Bridge at the northern end and Glenridding to the south. Management plans in the past have been valley based: Ullswater is no exception, with the first management plan being agreed in 1973 and revised in 1989. At the time of the preparation of the first plan, there was a public right of navigation on the Lake. The plan proposed the introduction of a speed limit which finally came into force in 1983 after being made in 1978. The speed limit effectively stopped water skiing on the Lake. Launch facilities are limited to one public slipway and a number of private access points at campsites and marinas. However the amount of water activity, particularly windsurfing, appears to have levelled off in the 1990s. The peak count occurred in 1987 with 500 craft in use on the Lake and a further 400 moored. That peak has not been reached since, with 324 boats in use and 471 moored at the last census in 1994.

Ownership of the Lake is divided between Dalesmain estate and the National Park with a small area owned by the National Trust. Moorings on the Lake are controlled by the National Park through their planning powers as well as through their ownership of a proportion of the 320 moorings on the Lake. Land ownership around the Lake includes the Dalesmain, Greystoke and Lowther estates as well as the National Trust and the National Park Authority. The latter owns a farm on the east side of the Lake with a mile of Lake foreshore. The farm is tenanted but is used for educational use. A major reason for purchase is the nature conservation value of two woodlands on the farm, both of which are designated as SSSIs.

The National Park also manages an area of foreshore on the eastern side where there is direct access from the road. Lay-bys for up to 112 cars have been provided to overcome uncontrolled car parking along the roadside. The lease allows access for informal purposes to the water and the Park

Authority has undertaken erosion control and revegetation. Lease costs are £500 per year (compared to £1 in 1961) and erosion control costs around £2,000 a year.

There is a steamer service on Ullswater but it only calls at three points—Glenridding and Pooley Bridge, and an intermediate stop at How Town. Many visitors travel from Glenridding to How Town and walk back along the lake shore. Over 700 people a day have been counted on the path. The management plan is looking at the possibility of opening a fourth landing point at Aira Force, a popular waterfall site owned by the National Trust.

A final issue is sewage control. Currently there is no bylaw requiring sealed toilets on boats using the lake and no requirement on the steamers to use pump out facilities. Following algal blooms, the yacht club have now installed a pump out facility while the steamer company is also prepared to install such a facility on their own jetty.

The Group then proceeded to Penrith station at the end of the visit. En route, *Bob Cartwright* summed up the main points of the visit. He emphasised that problems should be seen in perspective, that the Park is still very attractive, and that the Park Authority has tried to develop links with other partners to pool efforts, skills and resources, concentrating recently on a negotiated management approach to the problems of mountain biking and off-road vehicles.

SUMMARY TABLE:
REFERENCES

1. Note: the figures for governing body membership and estimated popularity for different sports are not directly comparable, as they have been produced on different dates and calculated on different criteria (for example, a minority of the figures below cover England only, rather than the UK). It is worth noting that the governing bodies for some sports, for example shooting, are likely to have a greater proportion of participants as members because licences have to be issued through them compared to activities such as walking where only a minority of those who participate become involved with the governing body. For a more detailed appraisal of this issue, see the introduction to "A Digest of Sports Statistics for the UK" (Sports Council) Third Edition 1991.

2. Ev p. 234.

3. Countryside Sports and the Watling Chase Community Forest, PA Cambridge Economic Consultants Limited, July 1993.

4. Target Group Index, copyright BMRB 1994.

5. General Household Survey 1993.

6. MORI survey (July 1993).

7. UK Domestic Visits Survey 1993: Ev pp. 7, 123.

8. Ev p. 110

9. Ev p. 199, Ap 42 para 2.4.2.

10. Q468.

11. QQ696, 702, Ev pp. 155, 200, 253, Ap 42 para 2.2.

12. Ev p. 254.

13. Q698.

14. Ev p. 236.

15. Q696

16. Q711

17. Q722

18. May 1995

19. Target Group Index, copyright BMRB 1994.

20. Urban and rural. General Household Survey 1993.

21. Ev p. 110.

22. Ev p. 199, Ap 42.

23. Ev p. 253.

24. Q516, Ap 29, Letter from John Burry, Official Verderer, to the Deputy Surveyor of the New Forest (Ev not printed).

25. Q259.

26. Ap 23.

27. *Ibid.*

28. Frederick Whitehead (Ev not printed).

29. Ap 23.

30. *Ibid.*

31. *Ibid*

32. May 1995

33. Urban and rural activity; General Household Survey 1993

34. Ev p. 199, Ap 42 para 2.4.2.

35. Q738.

36. *Ibid*

37. Ev p. 110.

38. Ev p. 199.

39. Ap 42 para 3.6.1.

40. Ev p. 139.

41. Ev p. 253.

42. Ap 24 para 7 (iv).

43. Q244

44. Ev p. 182

45. Q746

46. QQ749, 764.

47. Ev p. 254

48. Q738.

49. Ev p. 244.
50. Q765.
51. Ev p. 244.
52. Ap 25.
53. Target Group Index, copyright BMRB 1994.
54. General Household Survey 1993.
55. Q340.
56. Ev p. 110.
57. Q389.
58. Ap 45 para 2.1.
59. Q340.
60. Ap 25 page 2 para A (i).
61. Quote from Geoff Ball, Abstraction Control Manager, NRA, Thames Region (Ap 25).
62. 'Guidance Notes for Public Footpaths and Bridleways on New Golf Courses', English Golf Union.
63. Ap 25.
64. *Ibid.*
65. May 1995. United Kingdom membership, Caravan Club (Ev not printed).
66. As at October 31 1994 (figure from the Annual Accounts).
67. End of February 1995.
68. National Caravan Council (Ev not printed).
69. Target Group Index, copyright BMRB 1994.
70. Q340.
71. Ap 45 para 2.1.
72. Ap 29 Appendix 2 para 4.
73. British Holiday and Home Parks Association Limited (Ev not printed); National Caravan Council (Ev not printed).
74. British Holiday and Home Parks Association (Ev not printed)
75. *Ibid.*
76. The Environment and Development Company (Ev not printed)
77. Caravan Club (Ev not printed).
78. National Caravan Council Ltd (Ev not printed).
79. Great Britain and Northern Ireland, end of April 1995.
80. Annual membership for 1994.
81. Source: General Household Survey 1993.
82. Ev p. 110.
83. Ev p. 199, Ap 42 para 2.4.2.
84. Ap 42 para 2.4.9.
85. Ev p. 254.
86. Ap 6.
87. *Ibid.*
88. *Ibid.*
89. Ap 9.
90. General Household Survey 1993.
91. Target Group Index, copyright BMRB 1994.
92. Ev pp. 110 253.
93. Pembrokeshire Coast National Park (Ev not printed).
94. *Ibid.*
95. Ap 9.
96. *Ibid.*
97. *Ibid.*
98. *Ibid.*
99. Estimate by the National Caving Association, May 1995.
100. *Ibid.*
101. Ev p. 110.
102. Ap 35.
103. National Caving Association: Cave Conservation Policy 1995.
104. End of April 1995.
105. Ap 10.
106. Ev p. 110.
107. Q436.

108. Ap 10 Annex C.
109. Ap 10.
110. *Ibid.*
111. *Ibid.*
112. As of May 1915.
113. National Small-bore Rifle Association, National Rifle Association and the National Pistol Association NSRA as of May 1995, about 15,000 individuals and 1,200 clubs (they may or may not be affiliated). NPA as of May 1994, 1740 individual members, 429 clubs which vary in size.
114. Target Group Index, copyright BRMB 1994.
115. *Ibid.*
116. App 24.48. Mr W G Thomas (Ev not Printed).
117. Ap 112.
118. *Ibid.*
119. Ap 12, British Association for Shooting and Conservation (Ev not printed).
120. Ap 12.
121. *Ibid.*
122. *Ibid.*
123. Target Group Index, copyright BMRB 1994.
124. LARA supplementary evidence (not printed).
125. QQ449, 450.
126. Q584.
127. Ap 42 para 3.4.1.
128. LARA supplementary evidence (not printed).
129. *Ibid.*
130. As of May 1995.
131. Ap 42 para 3.4.1.
132. Ap 42 para 3.5.1.
133. Ap 24 para 7 (iv).
134. Ap 1.
135. *Ibid.*
136. *Ibid.*
137. Ap 3 para 1.2.
138. Ap 3 para 3.4.
139. Ap 3 para 6.1.
140. Ap 3 para 3.6
141. *Ibid.*
142. Ap 3 para 5.2.
143. The RYA has 75,000 personal members and 1,500 clubs, federations and class associations in affiliation. Total affiliated membership is "around half a million people".
144. General Household Survey 1993.
145. Target Group Index, copyright BMRB 1994.
146. *Ibid.*
147. General Household Survey 1993.
148. QQ338, 343.
149. Ap 45 para 2.1.
150. Ap 46.
151. British Marine Industries Federation (Ev not printed).
152. Ap 46.
153. Ev p. 126
154. Ap 46.
155. Ev p. 105.
156. Ap 38.
157. Pembrokeshire Coast National Park (Ev not printed)
158. Roger Lankester (Ev not printed).
159. British Marine Industries Federation (Ev not printed).
160. *Ibid.*
161. Ap 46.
162. Roger Lankester (Ev not printed).
163. General Household Survey 1993.
164. Ap 38.
165. Pembrokeshire Coast National Park (Ev not printed).

166. Ap 2.
167. *Ibid.*
168. *Ibid.*
169. As of May 1995 (approx).
170. Calculated on number sold balance of imports and breakdowns.
171. Figures supplied by Personal Watercraft Association.
172. Ap 38.
173. Q666.
174. Q611.
175. Ap 43.
176. *Ibid.*
177. *Ibid.*
178. *Ibid.*
179. Ev p. 219.
180. Ev p. 129 (Estimate by Leisure Consultants for the British Water Ski Federation).
181. Target Group Index, copyright BMRB 1994.
182. Ap 38.
183. Pembrokeshire Coast National Park (Ev not printed).
184. Q672.
185. Ev p. 218
186. Q664.
187. Q671.
188. Q681.
189. Q694.
190. In April 1994 there were 513 affiliated clubs with 221,699 members in England (this includes one Irish club).
191. The Salmon and Trout Association has 14,500 individual and trade members, and 270 member clubs. 100,000 is an estimate from the Association.
192. The NFSA has 1,800 personal members and 560 affiliated clubs. As of May 1995 they estimated that this accounted for in all 35,000 members.
193. General Household Survey 1993.
194. Target Group Index, copyright BMRB 1994.
195. *Ibid.*
196. *Ibid.*
197. Ap 38.
198. Ap 38, Pembrokeshire Coast National Park (Ev not printed).
199. Ap 38.
200. *Ibid.*
201. Ev p. 253.
202. Ap 37.
203. *Ibid* (quotation ascribed to David Bellamy).
204. *Ibid.*
205. *Ibid.*
206. Popular Flying Association (Ev not printed).
207. Ap 42 para 3.7.1.
208. Ap 28.
209. *Ibid.*
210. Ap 28, General Aviation Awareness Council (Ev not printed), Aircraft Owners and Pilots Association (Ev not printed), Popular Flying Association (Ev not printed).
211. Aircraft Owners and Pilots Association (Ev not printed).
212. Ap 28.
213. *Ibid.*
214. *Ibid.*
215. *Ibid.*
216. Popular Flying Association (Ev not printed).
217. National Farmers Union.
218. Q896.
219. Estimate supplied for May 1995 for Britain by the British Gliding Association.
220. Q895.
221. Ap 4.
222. *Ibid.*

223. *Ibid.*
224. *Ibid.*
225. *Ibid.*
226. *Ibid.*
227. *Ibid.*
228. Ap 5.
229. Ap 24 para 7 (iv).
230. Ap 25.
231. *Ibid.*
232. *Ibid.*
233. *Ibid.*
234. May 1995 (estimate).
235. Ap 42 para 3.7.1.
236. Ap 7.
237. Ap 7 (Which 'are frequently alleviated by simple demonstration flights').
238. Ap 7.
239. Ap 8.
240. Ap 24 para 7 (iv).
241. Ap 8.
242. *Ibid.*
243. *Ibid.*
244. *Ibid.*
245. European Paintball Sports Federation (Ev not printed); they note that there are three times that many sites in existence.
246. European Paintball Sports Federation. They note that it has been suggested recently that this figure be revised upward.
247. QQ431, 447.
248. European Paintball Sports Federation (Ev not printed).
249. *Ibid.*
250. May 1995.
251. Target Group Index, copyright BMRB 1994.
252. Ap 45 Annex 1; point 5, summary of the RSPB's recommendations for the consultation draft of the Poole Harbour Aquatic Management Plan.

EXTRACT FROM MINUTES OF PROCEEDINGS RELATING TO DECLARATIONS OF INTEREST

WEDNESDAY 29 MARCH 1995

The Chairman declared a non pecuniary interest in relation to the Committee's inquiry into the Environmental Impact of Leisure Activities as a member of The Ramblers' Association.

Mr Roy Thomason and Mr Den Dover each declared a non pecuniary interest in relation to the Committee's inquiry into the Environmental Impact of Leisure Activities as a Vice President of the Association of District Councils.

WEDNESDAY 3 MAY 1995
[Morning Meeting]

Mr Clifton-Brown declared a non pecuniary interest in relation to the Committee's inquiry into the Environmental Impact of Leisure Activities as a member of the Country Landowners Association.

WEDNESDAY 3 MAY 1995
[Afternoon meeting]

Mr Clifton-Brown declared a non pecuniary interest in relation to the Committee's inquiry into the Environmental Impact of Leisure Activities as a member of the National Farmers' Union.

PROCEEDINGS OF THE COMMITTEE
RELATING TO CONSIDERATION OF THE REPORT

WEDNESDAY 12 JULY 1995

Members present:

Mr Andrew F Bennett, in the Chair.

Mr Geoffrey Clifton-Brown	Helen Jackson
Mr John Denham	Mr Bill Olner
Mr Den Dover	Mr Michael Stephen
Mr Harold Elletson	Mr Roy Thomason

The Committee deliberated.

Draft Report (The Environmental Impact of Leisure Activities), proposed by the Chairman, brought up and read.

Ordered, That the Report be read a second time, paragraph by paragraph.

Paragraphs 1 to 190 read and agreed to.

Summary of recommendations and conclusions read and agreed to.

Ordered, That Annexes I, II, III, IV, V and VI be appended to the Report.

Resolved, That the Report, as amended, be the Fourth Report of the Committee to the House. Ordered, That the Chairman do make the Report to the House.

Ordered, That the provisions of Standing Order No. 116 (Select Committees (reports)) be applied to the Report.

Several papers were ordered to be appended to the Minutes of Evidence.

Ordered, That the Appendices to the Minutes of Evidence be reported to the House.—*(The Chairman.)*

Several Memoranda were ordered to be reported to the House.

[Adjourned till Wednesday 19 July at a quarter past Nine o'clock.

Printed in the United Kingdom by HMSO
19585 C11 7/95 216069
CRC supplied

ISBN 0-10-271695-1